PORTO AND LISBON TRAVEL GUIDE 2025

Explore Portugal's Iconic Cities Through Hidden Gems and Local Delights

PATRICK M. FINKEL

Copyright Notice

Copyright © [2024] [Patrick M. Finkel]. All Rights Reserved.

This publication and its contents, including but not limited to text, graphics, images, and any other material, are the intellectual property of [Author's Name] and are protected by applicable copyright laws and international treaties. Unauthorized use, reproduction, duplication, distribution, modification, transmission, or storage in any form or by any means, whether electronic, mechanical, or otherwise, is strictly prohibited without the express written consent of the copyright holder.

This prohibition includes, but is not limited to, the unauthorized uploading, sharing, or hosting of this material on any digital platform, website, or social media channel, as well as the use of this work for commercial purposes without permission. The creation of derivative works or translations of this publication is also prohibited without prior authorization.

Permissions for use beyond the scope of this copyright notice must be obtained in writing from [Patrick M. Finkel]. For inquiries regarding permissions, licensing, or authorized uses, please contact: [abbadigitalhandle@gmail.com].

The author retains all moral and intellectual rights to this work, ensuring its integrity and proper attribution. Violators of these rights will be subject to civil and criminal penalties to the fullest extent of the law.

Note: This book doesn't contain many images. Readers are advised to concentrate on the text to explore useful information within the book and scan the Qr codes for Locating various places.

TABLE OF CONTENTS

Introduction..7
   Welcome to Portugal.. 7
   Why Visit Porto and Lisbon?.. 9
   How to Use This Guide.. 10

Chapter 1: Planning Your Trip...13
   Best Times to Visit... 13
   Essential Travel Documents.. 14
   Budgeting and Costs.. 16
   Packing Tips for Portugal... 20

Chapter 2: Getting to Portugal...23
   Flights and Airports in Porto.. 23
   Flights and Airports in Lisbon.. 25
   Train and Bus Options in Porto.. 29
   Train and Bus Options in Lisbon... 32

Chapter 3: Getting Around..37
   Public Transportation in Lisbon and Porto.. 37
   Renting a Car vs. Using Taxis and Ride-Sharing................................ 40
   Navigating by Foot and Bicycle... 44

Chapter 4: Accommodation Options... 49
   Top Hotels and Boutique Stays in Porto.. 49
   Top Hotels and Boutique Stays in Lisbon... 54
   Budget-Friendly Hostels in Porto... 59
   Budget-Friendly Hostels in Lisbon.. 62
   Family and Group-Friendly Rentals... 66

Chapter 5: Cultural Insights 69
   Language Basics and Useful Phrases 69
   Customs and Etiquette in Portugal 73
   Local Festivals and Events in Porto and Lisbon 76

Chapter 6: Porto: The Invincible City 81
   Top Attractions in Porto 81
   Exploring Ribeira and the Douro River 86
   Gastronomic Delights in Porto 88
   Day Trips from Porto 92

Chapter 7: Lisbon: The City of Light 97
   Must-See Landmarks in Lisbon 97
   Hidden Gems and Local Neighborhoods in Lisbon 102
   Where to Eat in Lisbon 105
   Top Day Trips from Lisbon 109

Chapter 8: Outdoor and Adventure Activities 113
   Beaches Near Porto and Lisbon 113
   Hiking Trails and Nature Escapes 116
   Wine Tours and Tastings 119

Chapter 9: Food and Drink in Portugal 123
   Traditional Portuguese Dishes 123
   The Best Pastel de Nata Spots 126
   Iconic Wines and Ports in Portugal 129

Chapter 10: Shopping and Souvenirs 133
   Best Shopping Streets and Markets 133
   Unique Portuguese Handicrafts 136
   Where to Buy Authentic Tiles and Ceramics 140

chapter 11: Seasonal Travel Tips 143
   What to Expect in Each Season 143
   Seasonal Activities and Events 146
   Weather and Packing Advice 149

Chapter 12: Safety and Practical Information in Portugal................................ 153
   Health and Safety Tips.. 153
   Emergency Contacts and Services..156
   Staying Connected (Wi-Fi, SIM Cards).. 159

Chapter 13: Itineraries and Recommendations... 163
   3-Day Itinerary for First-Time Visitors... 163
   One Week in Porto and Lisbon..166
   Family-Friendly Itineraries for Porto and Lisbon... 169
   Useful Websites and Apps For Traveling to Portugal.. 172

SCAN THE QR CODE TO LOCATE PORTUGAL

Introduction

Welcome to Portugal

Portugal is a country that has charmed travelers for centuries, thanks to its rich history, vibrant culture, stunning landscapes, and warm hospitality. Nestled in the southwestern corner of Europe, Portugal is a land of contrasts—where modernity seamlessly blends with tradition, and every corner tells a story of its past. From the cobbled streets of Porto to the sun-kissed shores of Lisbon, this nation offers an unforgettable experience for every traveler.

For first-time visitors, Portugal can feel like stepping into a postcard. Its cities are brimming with architectural marvels, from centuries-old castles and monasteries to pastel-colored houses perched on hillsides. Lisbon, the capital, radiates charm with its iconic yellow trams, vibrant street art, and sweeping views of the Tagus River. Porto, the country's second-largest city, is equally enchanting, with its riverside Ribeira district, historic wine cellars, and the magnificent Dom Luís I Bridge. Both cities are steeped in history yet offer the vibrancy of contemporary European life.

What truly sets Portugal apart is its welcoming people. Known for their warmth and friendliness, the Portuguese are proud of their heritage and are often eager to share their culture with visitors. Whether you're learning about the traditional art of Fado music, savoring a meal of freshly grilled sardines, or sipping a glass of Port wine in a centuries-old cellar, you'll find that hospitality is at the heart of every Portuguese experience.

Beyond the urban centers, Portugal's natural beauty is nothing short of breathtaking. The country's diverse geography ranges from golden beaches along the Atlantic coast to rolling vineyards in the Douro Valley and lush mountains in the north. Each region has its own distinct character and allure. Whether you're hiking the trails of the Sintra-Cascais Natural Park, exploring the sun-drenched Algarve, or taking a leisurely boat ride down the Douro River, Portugal's landscapes will leave you in awe.

Portugal is also a paradise for food lovers. The cuisine is a reflection of the country's maritime heritage, with fresh seafood playing a starring role. Don't miss the chance to try a bowl of caldo verde, Portugal's beloved green soup, or indulge in a warm pastel de nata, the famous custard tart that has won hearts worldwide.

Welcome to Porto

As you prepare to embark on your journey, know that Portugal is more than just a destination, it's an experience that will stay with you long after you leave. With its captivating beauty, rich traditions, and warm-hearted people, Portugal is ready to welcome you with open arms. Whether you're a seasoned traveler or venturing abroad for the first time, this is a country that promises to inspire and enchant at every turn.

Why Visit Porto and Lisbon?

Porto and Lisbon are two of Europe's most captivating cities, each offering a unique blend of history, culture, and modern charm. Together, they encapsulate the best of Portugal, providing travelers with a well-rounded experience of the country's heritage, cuisine, and breathtaking landscapes. Here's why these iconic cities should top your travel list:

1. Rich History and Architecture
Both Porto and Lisbon boast a fascinating past that stretches back centuries. In Lisbon, you'll find landmarks like the Jerónimos Monastery and the Tower of Belém, both UNESCO World Heritage Sites, showcasing Portugal's maritime legacy. The city's Alfama district, with its narrow, winding streets, is a window into medieval times. In Porto, the Ribeira district transports you to another era with its colorful, tiled facades and cobblestone streets. Don't miss the stunning Livraria Lello bookstore, often cited as one of the most beautiful in the world, or the opulent interiors of the Bolsa Palace.

2. Unparalleled Scenic Beauty
Lisbon is known for its hills, offering panoramic views from iconic spots like Miradouro da Senhora do Monte and the São Jorge Castle. The Tagus River adds to the city's allure, providing picturesque settings for leisurely strolls or sunset cruises. Porto, on the other hand, is defined by the Douro River. The views from the Dom Luís I Bridge are spectacular, especially at sunset, and the rolling hills of the Douro Valley nearby make for a perfect day trip.

3. Culinary Delights
Portugal is a haven for food lovers, and these two cities offer culinary experiences that are second to none. In Lisbon, indulge in fresh seafood dishes like bacalhau à brás (salt cod) or savor a warm pastel de nata from the original Pastéis de Belém. Porto, meanwhile, is synonymous with Port wine. Tour the wine cellars of Vila Nova de Gaia and enjoy tastings paired with traditional dishes like francesinha, a hearty sandwich covered in a rich, spicy sauce.

4. Vibrant Culture and Traditions

Both cities are cultural hubs, offering everything from world-class museums to traditional Fado music performances. Lisbon's modern art scene and street art are as captivating as its historic charm, while Porto's artisanal crafts, like the famous azulejos (ceramic tiles), celebrate Portuguese traditions.

5. Accessibility and Diversity

Lisbon and Porto are well-connected by modern transportation, making them easy to explore. Despite their proximity, the two cities offer distinct atmospheres. Lisbon feels vibrant and cosmopolitan, while Porto exudes a more relaxed and traditional vibe. Together, they offer a diverse experience, appealing to travelers of all tastes.

Whether you're drawn to history, food, scenic beauty, or vibrant culture, Porto and Lisbon promise unforgettable memories. These cities are more than just destinations, they're an invitation to experience the heart and soul of Portugal.

How to Use This Guide

This travel guide is designed to help you make the most of your visit to Porto and Lisbon, whether it's your first time in Portugal or you're returning to explore these iconic cities in greater depth. With a focus on practical advice and insider tips, this guide is your go-to companion for planning, navigating, and experiencing the best that these two cities have to offer.

1. Tailor Your Experience

The guide is divided into clear sections, so you can easily find information that matches your travel needs. Planning your trip? Head to the **Planning Your Trip** section for tips on budgeting, packing, and timing your visit. Looking for specific attractions or activities? Explore the dedicated sections on **Porto** and **Lisbon** to discover top landmarks, hidden gems, and must-try experiences.

2. Navigate With Ease

Whether you're arriving by plane, train, or bus, the **Getting to Portugal** and **Getting Around** sections provide all the details you need to make your journey stress-free. Once you're in the cities, you'll find tips for using public transportation, walking routes, and even cycling paths to help you get around like a local.

3. Plan Day by Day
This guide offers suggested itineraries tailored to different types of travelers. Whether you're visiting for a weekend, a week, or longer, check out the **Itineraries and Recommendations** section for well-planned routes that combine iconic landmarks, dining spots, and local experiences.

4. Immerse Yourself in Culture
For those who love delving into the culture of their destination, the **Cultural Insights** and **Food and Drink** sections are invaluable. Learn about local customs, festivals, and Portuguese cuisine, so you can truly appreciate the unique character of Porto and Lisbon.

5. Be Prepared for Every Season
The **Seasonal Travel Tips** section ensures that you're ready for any time of year. Whether you're visiting in the sunny summer months or during Portugal's cooler seasons, you'll find advice on what to expect and how to pack.

6. Stay Safe and Connected
Traveling is always more enjoyable when you feel secure and prepared. The **Safety and Practical Information** section covers everything from emergency contacts to tips on staying connected with Wi-Fi and local SIM cards.

7. Make It Your Own
This guide is meant to be flexible and adaptable. While it provides a wealth of recommendations, feel free to customize your experience based on your interests, pace, and preferences.

With this guide, you'll have everything you need to explore Porto and Lisbon confidently, efficiently, and with the curiosity of a local. Whether you're chasing iconic sights, indulging in Portuguese delicacies, or uncovering hidden corners of the cities, this guide is here to make your adventure unforgettable.

Overview of Lisbon

Chapter 1: Planning Your Trip

Best Times to Visit

LllPortugal's mild climate makes Porto and Lisbon ideal destinations year-round, but certain times of the year offer unique experiences depending on your preferences. Whether you're looking to explore cultural festivals, enjoy sunny weather, or avoid crowds, here's a breakdown of the best times to visit these two iconic cities:

1. Spring (March to May)
Spring is one of the best times to visit Porto and Lisbon. The weather is warm but not overly hot, making it perfect for outdoor activities and sightseeing. Parks and gardens bloom with colorful flowers, adding a vibrant touch to the cities. Tourist crowds are manageable during this period, and prices for accommodation and flights are generally lower compared to the summer months.

- **Highlights**: Cherry blossoms in Lisbon's parks, pleasant temperatures for walking tours in Porto, and Easter festivities.
- **Average Temperatures**: 15–20°C (59–68°F).

2. Summer (June to August)
Summer is peak tourist season in Portugal. Both cities come alive with festivals, open-air events, and vibrant nightlife. The days are long and sunny, making it ideal for exploring beaches near Lisbon or enjoying river cruises along the Douro in Porto. However, the popularity of this season means higher prices for accommodations and more crowded attractions.

- **Highlights**: Santo António Festival in Lisbon (June), São João Festival in Porto (June), and beach getaways.
- **Average Temperatures**: 25–30°C (77–86°F).

3. Autumn (September to November)
Autumn offers a sweet spot for travelers. The weather remains warm, but the summer crowds begin to thin out. The grape harvest season in the Douro Valley, near Porto, is a unique experience, and Lisbon's sunsets during autumn are particularly breathtaking. This is also a great time for food lovers, as many local culinary festivals take place during this season.

- **Highlights**: Douro Valley wine harvest tours, milder weather, and fewer crowds.
- **Average Temperatures**: 15–25°C (59–77°F).

4. Winter (December to February)

Winter is the quietest season for tourism in Porto and Lisbon, but it has its own charm. The weather is mild compared to other European destinations, and you'll enjoy lower prices and shorter lines at major attractions. This is also the season for Christmas markets and holiday lights, which add a magical touch to the cities.

- **Highlights**: Holiday festivities, fewer tourists, and opportunities to explore museums and indoor attractions without the rush.
- **Average Temperatures**: 10–15°C (50–59°F).

When to Visit Based on Preferences:

- **For sunny weather and vibrant festivals**: Visit in summer.
- **For fewer crowds and pleasant weather**: Choose spring or autumn.
- **For budget travel and cozy experiences**: Winter is your best bet.

No matter when you visit, Porto and Lisbon have something special to offer. Each season brings its own unique vibe, ensuring an unforgettable experience at any time of the year.

Essential Travel Documents

When visiting Porto and Lisbon, ensuring you have the correct travel documents is crucial for a hassle-free trip. Here's a comprehensive list of the essentials to help you prepare:

1. Passport

A valid passport is required for all international travelers entering Portugal. Make sure your passport:

- Has at least six months of validity remaining from your date of entry.
- Contains enough blank pages for entry and exit stamps.

2. Visa (if applicable)
Portugal is part of the Schengen Area, so visa requirements depend on your nationality:

- **No visa required**: Citizens of the European Union, Schengen Area countries, and several other nations (e.g., the United States, Canada, Australia, and the UK) can enter Portugal for tourism for up to 90 days without a visa.
- **Visa required**: Travelers from non-exempt countries must obtain a Schengen visa in advance. Check with your local Portuguese consulate or embassy for application requirements.

3. Proof of Accommodation
Immigration officials may request evidence of where you'll be staying. This could be:

- Hotel reservations.
- A letter of invitation from a host (if staying with friends or family).

4. Return or Onward Ticket
Some travelers may be asked to show proof of a return flight or onward travel plans to ensure you're not overstaying the allowed period.

5. Travel Insurance
While not always mandatory, travel insurance is highly recommended. If you require a Schengen visa, insurance is a requirement and must:

- Cover at least €30,000 for medical expenses and emergency repatriation.
- Be valid for the entire Schengen Area and for the duration of your trip.

6. COVID-19 Requirements (If Applicable)
Depending on current regulations, travelers may need:

- Proof of vaccination, a negative COVID-19 test, or a certificate of recovery.
- Masks for public transportation or specific venues (check current guidelines before departure).

7. Identification (For EU Travelers)
EU nationals can enter Portugal with a national ID card instead of a passport. Ensure your ID is valid and in good condition.

8. Driver's License

If you plan to rent a car, bring:

- Your home country's driver's license.
- An International Driving Permit (IDP) if your license is not in English or Portuguese (required for some non-EU licenses).

9. Financial Proof

Though rarely requested, be prepared to show you have sufficient funds for your stay. This can be in the form of:

- Bank statements.
- Credit cards or cash.

10. Copies of Important Documents

It's always wise to have digital and physical copies of your essential documents, such as:

- Passport and visa.
- Travel insurance policy.
- Flight and accommodation details.

By ensuring you have these documents in order, you'll avoid unnecessary delays and enjoy a smooth and worry-free journey to Porto and Lisbon.

Budgeting and Costs

Portugal, including its iconic cities of Porto and Lisbon, is known for being one of Europe's more affordable destinations. However, your travel budget can vary significantly depending on your travel style, preferences, and the time of year. Here's a detailed breakdown of the typical costs and budgeting tips to help you plan your trip.

1. Accommodation Costs

Your choice of lodging will heavily influence your overall expenses.

- **Budget Options**: Hostels and budget hotels offer dorm rooms or simple private accommodations starting at €15–€40 per night.
- **Mid-Range Options**: Boutique hotels, comfortable guesthouses, and Airbnb apartments range between €60–€120 per night.

- **Luxury Options**: High-end hotels or historic stays in restored palaces can cost €150–€400 per night or more.

Tips:

- Book early, especially during the summer and festival seasons, to secure better prices.
- Look for deals in less touristy neighborhoods or consider nearby towns for more affordable options.

---

2. Transportation Costs

Portugal has an efficient and affordable transportation system.

- **Public Transport in Cities**: A single tram or bus ticket costs around €1.50–€3.00, while daily passes are €6–€7.
- **Metro**: The metro in Lisbon is convenient and costs €1.65 per ride or €6.60 for a day pass. Porto's metro operates on a similar pricing system.
- **Taxis and Ride-Sharing**: Short rides within the city range from €6–€15. Apps like Bolt or Uber often provide cheaper alternatives to taxis.
- **Trains Between Cities**: Tickets between Lisbon and Porto range from €20–€35 for standard class. High-speed trains may cost slightly more but are faster and more comfortable.
- **Car Rentals**: Daily rental costs start at €25–€40, excluding fuel. Parking fees in city centers can add €10–€20 daily.

Tips:

- Purchase a rechargeable Viva Viagem card in Lisbon or the Andante card in Porto for cheaper public transport fares.
- Use long-distance buses for even more affordable intercity travel.

3. Food and Drink Costs

Portugal is a paradise for food lovers, and dining out can suit any budget.

- **Budget Meals**: Casual cafes and small eateries (tascas) offer meals for €6–€10. Look for daily specials (prato do dia).
- **Mid-Range Dining**: Restaurants serving traditional dishes cost around €15–€25 per person, including a drink.
- **Fine Dining**: High-end restaurants and Michelin-starred venues cost upwards of €50–€100 per person.
- **Drinks**: A coffee (espresso) is €1–€1.50, a glass of wine €3–€5, and a pint of beer €2.50–€4. A bottle of Port wine at a local shop costs €10–€20.

Tips:

- Save money by eating at local markets or bakeries for breakfast or snacks.
- Don't skip trying pastel de nata (custard tarts), often less than €1.50 each.

---

4. Attractions and Activities Costs

- **Museums and Monuments**: Entrance fees range from €5–€15 per site. Combo tickets and free entry days (often Sundays) can help reduce costs.
- **Tours**: Walking tours are often free (with tips encouraged), while guided wine cellar tours in Porto cost €15–€25.
- **Day Trips**: A day tour to Sintra, Cascais, or the Douro Valley can cost €50–€100, depending on the inclusions.

Tips:

- Research city passes like the Lisboa Card (from €21 for 24 hours), which includes free public transport and discounts on attractions.
- Explore free attractions like city viewpoints (miradouros) and historic neighborhoods.

---

5. Miscellaneous Costs

- **Shopping**: Souvenirs like cork products, azulejos (tiles), or Port wine range from €10–€50 depending on the quality.
- **Wi-Fi and SIM Cards**: SIM cards with data plans start at €10 for 5GB. Free Wi-Fi is common in hotels, cafes, and public spaces.
- **Tips and Gratuities**: Tipping is not mandatory but appreciated—leave 5–10% in restaurants or round up for taxis.

Daily Budget Estimates

- **Budget Traveler**: €40–€70/day
  - Dorm accommodation, public transport, street food, and free/low-cost attractions.
- **Mid-Range Traveler**: €100–€150/day
  - Comfortable hotels, casual dining, and occasional tours.
- **Luxury Traveler**: €200+/day
  - Luxury hotels, fine dining, private tours, and premium transportation.

Budgeting Tips

- **Travel Off-Season**: Visit during spring or autumn to save on flights and accommodations.
- **Eat Like a Local**: Opt for local eateries over tourist-oriented restaurants.
- **Book in Advance**: Early bookings often come with discounts on hotels, trains, and tours.
- **Use Free Resources**: Join free walking tours or explore the many free attractions in both cities.

By carefully planning your budget and taking advantage of these tips, you can enjoy everything Porto and Lisbon have to offer without breaking the bank!

Packing Tips for Portugal

Portugal's diverse climate, historic cities, and mix of urban and outdoor attractions call for thoughtful packing. Whether you're exploring the cobblestone streets of Porto, soaking up the sun in Lisbon, or venturing out to nearby day-trip destinations, here's everything you need to pack for a comfortable and enjoyable trip:

1. Clothing Essentials

Portugal has a Mediterranean climate, so packing layers is key to adapting to changing weather throughout the day.

- **Lightweight Layers**: Pack breathable shirts, dresses, and pants for daytime exploring, especially in spring and summer.
- **Warm Layers**: Bring a light jacket, sweater, or scarf for cooler evenings, especially in autumn or winter.
- **Comfortable Shoes**: The streets of Porto and Lisbon are famously steep and cobblestoned, so sturdy, comfortable walking shoes or sneakers are essential. Avoid heels unless they're block-heeled or wedge styles.
- **Rain Protection**: In winter or early spring, bring a compact umbrella or a waterproof jacket to prepare for occasional rain showers.
- **Seasonal Wear**:
    - Summer (June–August): Include lightweight clothing, a hat, and sunglasses to protect against the sun.
    - Winter (December–February): Pack a heavier jacket and possibly gloves for chillier evenings.

---

2. Travel Accessories

- **Daypack**: A small backpack or crossbody bag is perfect for carrying daily essentials like water, sunscreen, and your camera.
- **Reusable Water Bottle**: Tap water is safe to drink, and having a reusable bottle will save you money and reduce plastic waste.
- **Travel-Sized Toiletries**: Bring your own shampoo, conditioner, and skincare essentials in travel-sized containers. Portuguese pharmacies are well-stocked, but some brands may be unfamiliar.
- **Portable Charger**: Keep your phone or camera charged while exploring all day.

- **Plug Adapter**: Portugal uses Type C and Type F plugs with a 230V supply. If you're traveling from outside Europe, bring an appropriate adapter.

3. Documents and Money

- **Passport and Visa**: Ensure your passport is valid, and bring copies for backup.
- **Travel Insurance Information**: Have a printed and digital copy of your policy.
- **Credit/Debit Cards**: Most places accept cards, but carry some cash (euros) for smaller businesses or markets.
- **Guidebook or Digital App**: Bring this travel guide or a digital alternative for on-the-go references.

4. Tech and Gadgets

- **Phone and Charger**: Download maps, apps, and offline guides before arriving.
- **Camera**: Portugal's scenery is stunning, so bring a good-quality camera or make sure your phone camera is ready.
- **SIM Card or eSIM**: Purchase a local SIM card or eSIM for affordable data and calls.

5. Health and Comfort Items

- **Sunscreen and Lip Balm**: Essential for sunny days, especially in summer.
- **Medications**: Bring any prescription medications you need, along with a basic first aid kit (painkillers, plasters, and motion sickness tablets).
- **Anti-Chafing Cream**: Useful if you're walking long distances in warm weather.

6. Special Items for Portugal

- **Swimsuit and Beach Towel**: If you're visiting nearby beaches or coastal towns.
- **Wine Tote or Bottle Protector**: If you plan to bring back a bottle of Port wine from Porto.
- **Compact Binoculars**: Great for spotting views from Lisbon's miradouros (viewpoints) or during a Douro Valley river cruise.

7. Packing for Activities

- **For Sightseeing**: Comfortable clothes and shoes, a reusable water bottle, and a daypack.
- **For Day Trips**: Pack a lightweight rain jacket or sweater, depending on the season.
- **For Dining Out**: A smart-casual outfit for restaurants; locals tend to dress stylishly for evening outings.
- **For Hiking or Outdoor Adventures**: Sturdy walking shoes, moisture-wicking clothing, and a hat for sun protection.

Packing Tips

1. **Pack Light**: Portugal's cities are best explored on foot, and many accommodations lack elevators. Stick to a carry-on if possible.
2. **Use Packing Cubes**: Keep your belongings organized, especially if you're visiting multiple cities.
3. **Leave Room for Souvenirs**: Portugal is known for its ceramics, cork products, and Port wine, so save space in your luggage.
4. **Check the Weather Forecast**: Before you leave, verify the weather for your travel dates to ensure you're prepared.

By packing thoughtfully and planning for Portugal's unique charm and climate, you'll be ready to enjoy every moment of your trip to Porto and Lisbon!

Chapter 2: Getting to Portugal

Flights and Airports in Porto

Porto is served by **Francisco Sá Carneiro Airport** (also known as Porto Airport), which is one of Portugal's busiest and most modern international airports. Located approximately 11 kilometers (7 miles) northwest of Porto's city center, the airport is well-equipped to handle both domestic and international travelers. Here's everything you need to know about flights and navigating the airport:

1. Overview of Porto Airport (OPO)

- **Location**: Maia, about a 20–30-minute drive from Porto's city center.
- **Facilities**: The airport has a single terminal for both domestic and international flights. It features modern amenities, including shops, restaurants, currency exchange, and car rental services.
- **Airlines**:
  - Major carriers such as TAP Air Portugal, Ryanair, EasyJet, Lufthansa, and Air France operate here.
  - It's a hub for budget airlines, offering affordable flights to European destinations.

2. Flights to Porto

Porto Airport connects the city to various destinations worldwide, with a strong focus on European cities.

- **From Europe**:
  - Porto is well-connected to major hubs such as London, Paris, Madrid, Berlin, and Amsterdam.
  - Budget airlines like Ryanair and EasyJet frequently offer low-cost options.
- **From the Americas**:
  - Direct flights are available from some major cities, including New York and São Paulo, typically operated by TAP Air Portugal.
  - Connecting flights through Lisbon or Madrid are also common.

3. Transportation to and from Porto Airport

- **Metro**:
  - The easiest and most affordable option is the Metro Line E (Purple), which connects the airport to the city center in about 30 minutes. Tickets cost around €2–€3, including a small fee for the rechargeable Andante card.
- **Bus**:
  - Several public buses serve the airport, including lines 601, 602, and 604. These are cheaper but slower than the metro.
  - Private shuttle buses are also available, with fares starting around €5–€10.
- **Taxi and Ride-Sharing**:
  - Taxis are readily available, and a ride to the city center costs around €20–€30.
  - Ride-sharing apps like Uber, Bolt, and FreeNow typically offer slightly cheaper alternatives.
- **Car Rentals**:
  - Porto Airport has multiple car rental companies, making it a convenient option if you plan to explore the Douro Valley or other nearby regions.

---

4. Tips for Flying into Porto

1. **Book Early**: Especially during peak tourist seasons (summer and Christmas), flights to Porto can fill up quickly. Booking a few months in advance often secures better deals.
2. **Check Budget Airlines**: If you're traveling from Europe, Ryanair and EasyJet often have direct and inexpensive flights to Porto.
3. **Travel Light**: Budget airlines often have strict baggage policies. Pack efficiently to avoid additional fees.
4. **Check Layovers**: If you're connecting through Lisbon, be aware that the transfer time can vary depending on the airline. Allow at least 90 minutes for connections.
5. **Arrive Early**: Porto Airport is efficient, but during busy times, security lines can get long. Arrive 2–3 hours before international flights.

5. Airport Amenities and Services

- **Food and Drinks**: A variety of cafes, bars, and restaurants are available, offering Portuguese specialties and international cuisine.
- **Shopping**: Duty-free shops sell local products such as Port wine, ceramics, and souvenirs.
- **Wi-Fi**: Free Wi-Fi is available throughout the airport.
- **Lounges**: Premium lounges, such as ANA Lounge, offer comfort for travelers who want to relax before their flight.
- **Accessibility**: The airport is wheelchair-friendly, with elevators, ramps, and assistance available upon request.

---

6. Nearby Attractions for Layovers

If you have a long layover in Porto, the airport's proximity to the city center allows you to explore key attractions:

- Ribeira District (30 minutes away): Stroll along the Douro River and enjoy a scenic meal.
- Livraria Lello (30 minutes away): Visit one of the world's most beautiful bookstores.
- Clérigos Tower (30 minutes away): Climb for panoramic views of Porto.

Porto's Francisco Sá Carneiro Airport offers a seamless travel experience, with excellent connectivity, modern facilities, and efficient transportation options. Whether you're arriving from afar or hopping over from another European destination, it's the perfect gateway to begin your adventure in Porto.

Flights and Airports in Lisbon

Lisbon is served by **Humberto Delgado Airport** (commonly referred to as Lisbon Airport or Aeroporto de Lisboa), Portugal's largest and busiest airport. Conveniently located just 7 kilometers (4 miles) from Lisbon's city center, this modern airport acts as a major gateway for both international and domestic travelers. Here's everything you need to know about flights and navigating Lisbon Airport:

1. Overview of Lisbon Airport (LIS)

- **Location**: In the Camarate district, a short 15–20-minute drive from central Lisbon.
- **Terminals**:
    - **Terminal 1**: Handles most international flights and is the main terminal for departures and arrivals.
    - **Terminal 2**: Used primarily by low-cost carriers like Ryanair and EasyJet for departures only. A free shuttle bus connects the two terminals.
- **Facilities**: Lisbon Airport is equipped with modern amenities, including restaurants, shops, lounges, currency exchange services, and car rental offices.

---

2. Flights to Lisbon

As a major European hub, Lisbon Airport offers excellent connectivity to destinations worldwide:

- **From Europe**:
    - Lisbon is directly connected to most major European cities, including Paris, Madrid, London, Berlin, and Rome.
    - Budget airlines such as Ryanair, Wizz Air, and Vueling often operate here, alongside full-service carriers like TAP Air Portugal, British Airways, and Lufthansa.
- **From the Americas**:
    - Direct flights are available from key cities like New York, Miami, Toronto, and São Paulo, with airlines like TAP Air Portugal, Delta, and United Airlines.
    - Connecting flights through other European hubs are common for cities without direct routes.
- **From Africa**:
    - Lisbon has strong links to African nations, particularly those with historical ties to Portugal, such as Angola, Mozambique, and Cape Verde.
- **From Asia and Oceania**:
    - Travelers typically connect through hubs like Dubai (via Emirates), Doha (via Qatar Airways), or European cities like Frankfurt or Paris.

3. Transportation to and from Lisbon Airport

- **Metro**:
    - The **Red Line** connects the airport to the city center in about 20 minutes. A single ticket costs €1.65, plus €0.50 for the reusable Viva Viagem card.
- **Bus**:
    - Aerobus services offer a convenient connection between the airport and popular areas in Lisbon, with tickets costing €4–€5.
    - Regular public buses (lines 744, 783, and 208) are a cheaper alternative, but they can be crowded during peak hours.
- **Taxi and Ride-Sharing**:
    - A taxi ride to the city center costs approximately €10–€15.
    - Ride-sharing apps like Uber, Bolt, and FreeNow often provide more affordable options.
- **Car Rentals**:
    - Several car rental agencies operate at the airport, ideal for travelers planning to explore beyond Lisbon.
- **Train**:
    - While there's no direct train from the airport, you can connect to Lisbon's main train stations (Oriente or Rossio) via the metro or bus.

---

4. Tips for Flying into Lisbon

1. **Book Early**: Flights to Lisbon are in high demand, especially during summer and festival seasons. Booking early can save you money.
2. **Check Terminal Assignments**: If flying with low-cost carriers, confirm if your flight departs from Terminal 2 and allow extra time to reach it.
3. **Arrive Early**: Security lines can be lengthy during peak hours, so arrive at least 2–3 hours before international departures.
4. **Take Advantage of Layovers**: Lisbon Airport's proximity to the city makes it possible to explore attractions like the Alfama district, Praça do Comércio, or Belém Tower during long layovers.

5. Airport Amenities and Services

- **Dining Options**: Enjoy Portuguese specialties like pastéis de nata at local cafes, or opt for international cuisines.
- **Shopping**: From duty-free stores to local souvenir shops selling Portuguese wines, ceramics, and sardines.
- **Lounges**: Premium lounges like ANA Lounge and TAP Premium Lounge offer comfort and amenities for travelers.
- **Wi-Fi**: Free Wi-Fi is available throughout the airport.
- **Accessibility**: The airport is wheelchair-friendly, with elevators, ramps, and assistance available upon request.

---

6. Nearby Attractions for Layovers

Lisbon Airport is close enough to the city center to explore its highlights during a long layover:

- **Alfama**: Wander through this historic neighborhood, filled with narrow streets and Fado music venues.
- **Belém**: Visit iconic landmarks like the Jerónimos Monastery and the Belém Tower.
- **Baixa and Chiado**: Shop, dine, or enjoy a coffee in the heart of Lisbon.

---

7. Flights Beyond Lisbon

Lisbon Airport serves as a hub for exploring other Portuguese destinations:

- **Domestic Flights**: Direct flights to Porto, Faro, Madeira, and the Azores are frequent and convenient.
- **Connecting Flights**: TAP Air Portugal operates many connecting flights to Europe, Africa, and the Americas via Lisbon.

Lisbon Airport is a bustling, well-connected hub that offers travelers an efficient and enjoyable gateway to Portugal. Whether you're arriving, departing, or just passing through, the airport's amenities and proximity to the city make it an excellent starting point for your journey.

Train and Bus Options in Porto

Porto's public transportation network is efficient, affordable, and well-suited for both locals and travelers. Trains and buses offer excellent options for navigating the city and exploring nearby regions. Here's a detailed guide to train and bus options in Porto:

1. Train Options in Porto

Porto's train network includes both local and intercity services, making it easy to travel within the city and beyond.

Key Train Stations

1. **São Bento Station**:
    - A historic station located in the city center, known for its stunning azulejo (tile) artwork.
    - Primarily serves regional and suburban trains to nearby towns like Braga, Guimarães, and Aveiro.
2. **Campanhã Station**:
    - Porto's main train station for long-distance and high-speed trains.
    - Located a short metro or bus ride from the city center.
    - Serves Alfa Pendular (AP) and Intercidades (IC) trains connecting Porto with Lisbon, Coimbra, and the Algarve.

Types of Train Services

- **Urban and Regional Trains**:
    - Operated by Comboios de Portugal (CP), these connect Porto to nearby towns and cities.
    - Frequent, affordable, and ideal for day trips.
- **Intercity (IC) and Alfa Pendular (AP) Trains**:
    - These high-speed trains connect Porto to Lisbon, Coimbra, and other major destinations.
    - Tickets for these services should be booked in advance, especially during peak travel times.

Tips for Train Travel in Porto

- Use the **CP mobile app** to check schedules, book tickets, and view updates.
- Purchase a **Porto Card**, which includes discounts on regional train tickets.
- If taking the train to Lisbon, consider splurging on the Alfa Pendular for a more comfortable experience.

2. Bus Options in Porto

The bus network in Porto is extensive and a practical option for reaching areas not covered by the metro or train.

Key Bus Operators

1. **STCP (Sociedade de Transportes Colectivos do Porto)**:
   - The main operator of local buses in Porto.
   - Routes connect the city center to suburbs, parks, and attractions like Serralves Museum and Foz do Douro.
2. **Rede Expressos**:
   - Portugal's largest intercity bus operator, providing long-distance services to destinations across the country.
   - The Rede Expressos terminal in Porto is located at Campo 24 de Agosto.

Popular Bus Routes in Porto

- **500 Route**: Runs along the scenic Douro River from the city center to Matosinhos, a coastal town known for its beaches and seafood.
- **601 and 602 Routes**: Connect Porto city center to Francisco Sá Carneiro Airport.
- **Tourist Hop-On, Hop-Off Buses**: Operated by companies like Yellow Bus and City Sightseeing, these are ideal for quick overviews of Porto's main attractions.

Tips for Using Buses in Porto

- Purchase an **Andante card**, which can be loaded with credit for seamless travel on buses, trains, and metro.
- Check bus schedules online or through the **STCP mobile app**.
- Validate your ticket when boarding to avoid fines.

3. Intercity Travel from Porto

Both trains and buses are excellent options for exploring Portugal from Porto:

- **Trains**:
    - Porto to Lisbon: 2.5–3 hours via Alfa Pendular.
    - Porto to Braga or Guimarães: 1 hour via regional trains.
    - Porto to Coimbra: 1.5 hours via Intercidades or Alfa Pendular.
- **Buses**:
    - Rede Expressos buses are slower but often more affordable than trains.
    - Routes connect Porto to Lisbon, Fatima, Évora, and more.

---

4. Transportation Apps and Resources

- **CP - Comboios de Portugal**: For train schedules, tickets, and discounts.
- **STCP App**: For bus routes and live updates in Porto.
- **Moovit and Google Maps**: For real-time public transportation navigation.

---

5. Accessibility and Convenience

- **Accessibility**: Both trains and buses in Porto are generally wheelchair-accessible, but it's advisable to confirm specific needs in advance.
- **Cost**: Public transportation is affordable, with fares starting at €1.20 for a single bus or metro ride within Zone 1. Intercity travel costs vary based on distance and service type.

Porto's train and bus systems make it easy to navigate the city and explore its surroundings, whether you're heading to nearby beaches, the Douro Valley, or cities like Lisbon and Braga. Take advantage of these convenient options to enjoy all that Porto and the surrounding region have to offer!

Train and Bus Options in Lisbon

Lisbon boasts an extensive and efficient public transportation network, making it easy to navigate the city and explore nearby regions. Trains and buses are essential for both daily commutes and intercity travel, offering reliable and cost-effective options for locals and visitors alike. Here's a detailed guide to train and bus options in Lisbon:

1. Train Options in Lisbon

Lisbon's train network is operated primarily by **Comboios de Portugal (CP)** and offers connections within the city, the suburbs, and other regions of Portugal.

   Key Train Stations

   1. **Santa Apolónia Station**:
       - Located near the Alfama district, this is Lisbon's oldest railway station.
       - Serves regional, intercity, and international trains.
   2. **Oriente Station**:
       - A modern, well-connected hub in the Parque das Nações area.
       - Handles high-speed trains (Alfa Pendular) and intercity services, along with suburban lines.
   3. **Rossio Station**:
       - Centrally located in the Baixa district and known for its stunning Neo-Manueline architecture.
       - Primarily serves trains heading to Sintra.
   4. **Cais do Sodré Station**:
       - Located near the waterfront, this station connects to the Cascais Line for seaside destinations like Cascais and Estoril.

Types of Train Services

- **Suburban Trains:**
    - Operated by CP, these trains connect Lisbon to its suburbs and nearby towns, including Sintra, Cascais, and Azambuja.
    - Affordable and frequent, making them ideal for day trips.
- **Intercity and Alfa Pendular Trains**:
    - High-speed trains linking Lisbon to Porto, Coimbra, Faro, and other major cities.
    - These trains offer a faster, more comfortable option for long-distance travel.

Tips for Train Travel in Lisbon

- Use the **Viva Viagem card**, which can be loaded for both suburban trains and other public transport.
- Book tickets for long-distance trains in advance to secure better prices and preferred seating.
- For scenic routes, consider the train lines to Sintra or Cascais.

---

2. Bus Options in Lisbon

Lisbon's bus network is operated by **Carris**, which provides extensive coverage across the city, including areas not served by the metro or trains.

Key Bus Services

1. **Local Buses**:
    - Cover neighborhoods, hills, and attractions not accessible by metro, such as Belém and Bairro Alto.
    - Buses are frequent and operate from early morning until late at night.
2. **Airport Buses**:
    - Aerobus routes connect Lisbon Airport to key areas like Rossio, Praça do Comércio, and Cais do Sodré.
3. **Night Buses**:
    - Known as Rede da Madrugada, these buses operate between 11 PM and 6 AM, providing service when other transportation options are unavailable.
4. **Tourist Hop-On, Hop-Off Buses**:
    - Operated by companies like City Sightseeing and Yellow Bus Tours, these are ideal for a relaxed overview of Lisbon's main attractions.

Intercity and Regional Bus Services

- **Rede Expressos**:
    - The main operator for intercity buses, connecting Lisbon to cities like Porto, Coimbra, and Évora.
    - Tickets are affordable, and buses are equipped with Wi-Fi and air conditioning.
- **FlixBus**:
    - Offers budget-friendly intercity travel to various destinations in Portugal and Europe.

Tips for Using Buses in Lisbon

- Purchase a **Viva Viagem card** for seamless travel on buses, metro, and trams.
- Check schedules using the Carris app or Google Maps for real-time updates.
- Validate your ticket when boarding the bus to avoid fines.

---

3. Recommended Train and Bus Routes

- **Lisbon to Sintra (Train)**:
  - Duration: ~40 minutes from Rossio Station.
  - A must-do day trip to explore the fairytale-like palaces of Sintra.
- **Lisbon to Cascais (Train)**:
  - Duration: ~30 minutes from Cais do Sodré.
  - A scenic coastal route with views of the Atlantic.
- **Lisbon to Belém (Bus)**:
  - Take bus routes 727, 28, or 15E to visit iconic landmarks like the Jerónimos Monastery and Belém Tower.
- **Lisbon to Évora (Bus)**:
  - Duration: ~1.5 hours via Rede Expressos.
  - Explore this UNESCO-listed city known for its history and architecture.

---

4. Accessibility and Costs

- **Accessibility**:
  - Most trains and buses are wheelchair-friendly, but older vehicles or stations may have limitations. Check accessibility details before traveling.
- **Costs**:
  - A single bus ride within Lisbon costs approximately €1.50 with the Viva Viagem card.
  - Suburban train fares depend on the distance, starting at around €1.30.
  - Long-distance train tickets vary; early bookings can secure discounts.

---

5. Apps and Resources for Travel in Lisbon

- **CP App**: For train schedules, tickets, and updates.
- **Carris App**: For local bus routes and real-time tracking.
- **Google Maps and Moovit**: For integrated navigation across Lisbon's public transportation.

Lisbon's train and bus systems offer efficient, affordable, and scenic options for exploring the city and its surroundings. Whether you're heading to Sintra, Belém, or Cascais, these transportation modes ensure a seamless and enjoyable journey.

Chapter 3: Getting Around

Public Transportation in Lisbon and Porto

Lisbon and Porto boast efficient and affordable public transportation systems that make exploring these cities and their surroundings easy for both locals and visitors. Here's a detailed overview of public transportation options in these iconic Portuguese cities.

Public Transportation in Lisbon

Lisbon's network is operated primarily by **Carris (buses and trams)**, the **Metro**, and **Comboios de Portugal (trains)**.

1. Metro

- **Overview**: The Lisbon Metro is one of the fastest ways to get around. It features four color-coded lines (Blue, Yellow, Green, and Red) that connect the city center with suburbs and Lisbon Airport.
- **Key Tips**:
    - Operating Hours: 6:30 AM to 1:00 AM.
    - Cost: A single trip costs €1.65, or you can use the rechargeable **Viva Viagem card** for multiple rides.

2. Buses and Trams

- **Buses**: Operated by Carris, buses cover areas not served by the Metro, including historic neighborhoods like Alfama and Belém.
- **Trams**:
    - Famous trams like **Tram 28** offer a scenic route through Lisbon's narrow streets, passing iconic landmarks.
    - Tram rides cost €3 per trip or can be included with a Viva Viagem card.
- **Tips**: Validate your ticket when boarding to avoid fines.

3. Trains

- Suburban trains connect Lisbon to nearby destinations:
    - **Sintra Line**: From Rossio Station to the fairytale town of Sintra (~40 minutes).

- ○ **Cascais Line**: From Cais do Sodré to coastal towns like Cascais and Estoril (~30 minutes).
- Tickets: Fares depend on zones, starting at €1.30 with a Viva Viagem card.

4. Ferries

- Ferries operated by **Transtejo** and **Soflusa** connect Lisbon with cities across the Tagus River, such as Almada and Cacilhas.
- Popular Routes: Take a ferry to Cacilhas for stunning views of Lisbon's skyline.

Public Transportation in Porto

Porto's public transportation is well-organized, with the **Metro do Porto**, **buses**, **trams**, and **trains** forming the backbone of the network.

1. Metro

- Overview: Porto's Metro is a modern, efficient system with six lines (A to F) that connect the city center to suburbs and Porto Airport.
- **Key Tips**:
  - ○ Operating Hours: 6:00 AM to 1:00 AM.
  - ○ Cost: A single journey starts at €1.20, and the **Andante card** provides access to multiple zones.

2. Buses

- Operated by **STCP**, Porto's buses are extensive, covering areas the Metro does not reach.
- Cost: Around €1.20 per trip with an Andante card.

3. Historic Trams

- Porto's iconic trams offer a charming way to explore the city:
  - ○ **Tram 1**: Runs along the Douro River, from Ribeira to Foz do Douro.
  - ○ **Tram 22**: Circles the historic center.
  - ○ Cost: €3.50 per ride or €8 for a daily pass.

4. Trains

- Suburban trains connect Porto to nearby towns:
    - **São Bento Station**: For trips to Guimarães, Braga, and Aveiro.
    - **Campanhã Station**: For high-speed Alfa Pendular and intercity trains.
- Tickets: Start at €1.30 for suburban routes, depending on the distance.

Similarities Between Lisbon and Porto

- **Contactless Cards**: Both cities use rechargeable cards for seamless travel (Viva Viagem in Lisbon and Andante in Porto).
- **Affordability**: Public transportation is economical, with passes offering unlimited travel options.
- **Accessibility**: Both networks have wheelchair-accessible stations and vehicles, although older trams may pose challenges.
- **Scenic Options**: Historic trams in Lisbon and Porto provide picturesque routes through the cities.

Differences Between Lisbon and Porto

1. **Metro Coverage**:
    - Lisbon's Metro is larger and more comprehensive.
    - Porto's Metro extends further into suburban areas.
2. **Historic Trams**:
    - Lisbon's Tram 28 is more famous and widely used by tourists.
    - Porto's tram routes are fewer but offer scenic riverside views.
3. **River Ferries**:
    - Lisbon has ferries across the Tagus River, while Porto has bridges and boat tours on the Douro River.

Transportation Passes

- **Lisbon**:
    - **24-Hour Pass**: Unlimited travel on Metro, buses, trams, and ferries for €6.60.
    - Viva Viagem card can be reloaded for pay-as-you-go travel.

- **Porto**:
  - **Andante 24-Hour Pass**: Unlimited travel within selected zones starting at €4.15.
  - Andante Tour card for unlimited travel for 1 or 3 days (€7 or €15).

Public transportation in Lisbon and Porto is convenient and cost-effective, ensuring you can explore both cities with ease. Whether you're commuting locally, visiting nearby attractions, or just enjoying the journey, these systems provide reliable options for every traveler.

Renting a Car vs. Using Taxis and Ride-Sharing

Deciding between renting a car, taking taxis, or using ride-sharing services depends on your travel plans, preferences, and the locations you want to explore. Here's a detailed breakdown to help you make an informed decision.

Renting a Car in Portugal

Renting a car is an excellent option for travelers planning to explore areas outside Lisbon and Porto, such as the Algarve, Douro Valley, or Sintra.

Pros of Renting a Car

1. **Freedom and Flexibility**:
   - Travel at your own pace and visit remote locations not accessible by public transport.
2. **Ideal for Day Trips**:
   - Convenient for exploring smaller towns like Óbidos, Évora, or Nazaré.
3. **Cost-Efficient for Groups**:
   - Splitting the cost of a rental car and fuel among multiple travelers can be economical.
4. **Scenic Drives**:
   - Portugal offers stunning drives, such as along the Atlantic coast or through the Douro wine region.

Cons of Renting a Car

1. **Parking Challenges**:
    - In Lisbon and Porto, parking can be expensive and hard to find, especially in historic areas.
2. **Traffic and Tolls**:
    - Navigating city traffic can be stressful, and highways often have tolls.
3. **Cost**:
    - Rental costs, insurance, fuel, and tolls can add up, especially during peak seasons.
4. **Driving Restrictions**:
    - Narrow streets in historic districts like Alfama in Lisbon may not be accessible by car.

Cost Overview

- Daily rental: €25–€80 (depending on the car type and season).
- Fuel: €1.80–€2.00 per liter.
- Toll roads: Rates vary, but some roads can cost €10–€20 for long distances.

Tips for Renting a Car

- Opt for a **GPS** or use a navigation app to avoid getting lost.
- Consider renting a small car to navigate narrow streets and conserve fuel.
- Book in advance for better deals, especially during peak seasons.

Taxis in Portugal

Taxis are a convenient option for short trips, especially within cities or to/from airports.

Pros of Taxis

1. **Availability**:
    - Readily available in major cities and at transportation hubs.
2. **No Need for Parking**:
    - Ideal for getting around urban areas without worrying about parking.
3. **Convenient for Short Distances**:
    - Efficient for short trips, especially when carrying luggage or traveling late at night.

Cons of Taxis

1. **Cost**:
   - More expensive than public transport, especially for longer distances.
2. **Language Barrier**:
   - Some drivers may not speak fluent English, so having your destination written down helps.
3. **Limited Availability in Rural Areas**:
   - Outside of major cities, taxis may be harder to find.

Cost Overview

- Base fare: ~€3.50 during the day, ~€4.00 at night.
- Per kilometer: ~€0.47–€0.80.
- Airport surcharge: ~€1.60.

Tips for Using Taxis

- Always ask for a receipt to ensure you're charged correctly.
- Use official taxis (beige-colored with a roof light) to avoid scams.

Ride-Sharing Services in Portugal

Ride-sharing platforms like **Uber**, **Bolt**, and **Free Now** are popular and widely used in Lisbon, Porto, and other major cities.

Pros of Ride-Sharing

1. **Ease of Use**:
   - Book rides directly through an app, with transparent pricing and no need for cash.
2. **Affordable for Short Rides**:
   - Often cheaper than taxis for short urban trips.
3. **Reliable in Urban Areas**:
   - Widely available in cities and ideal for door-to-door service.

Cons of Ride-Sharing

1. **Limited in Rural Areas**:
   - Ride-sharing services are less common outside of major cities.
2. **Surge Pricing**:
   - Prices can increase significantly during peak hours or high demand.
3. **Dependence on Internet Access**:
   - Requires a smartphone and a stable internet connection.

Cost Overview

- Base fare: €1–€2.50.
- Per kilometer: €0.40–€0.60.
- Average city ride: €6–€12.

Tips for Using Ride-Sharing

- Compare prices between apps to find the best deal.
- Check the estimated wait time before booking, especially during busy periods.

Comparison: Renting a Car vs. Taxis and Ride-Sharing

Factor	Renting a Car	Taxis	Ride-Sharing
Best For	Day trips and rural exploration	Short trips in cities	Urban transportation
Cost	Higher upfront costs	Moderate, higher than apps	Affordable for short rides
Flexibility	Maximum flexibility	Limited to driver availability	Flexible, app-dependent
Parking Needed	Yes	No	No
Availability	Nationwide	Mostly in cities	Widely available in cities

Final Recommendations

- **Rent a Car**:
    - If you plan to explore regions like the Douro Valley, the Algarve, or small towns off the beaten path.
- **Use Taxis**:
    - For quick and hassle-free transportation in cities or for airport transfers.
- **Opt for Ride-Sharing**:
    - For affordable, convenient urban travel in Lisbon, Porto, and surrounding areas.

Choose based on your itinerary, budget, and preference for convenience or adventure!

Navigating by Foot and Bicycle

Both Lisbon and Porto are walkable cities with plenty to offer for pedestrians and cyclists. Exploring by foot or bicycle allows you to soak in the atmosphere, discover hidden gems, and enjoy Portugal's charm at your own pace. However, each city has unique challenges and rewards for those who choose to explore this way.

Navigating by Foot

Lisbon

1. **Why Walk in Lisbon?**
    - Lisbon's neighborhoods, like Alfama, Bairro Alto, and Chiado, are best experienced on foot due to their historic charm and narrow streets.
    - Walking lets you discover local cafes, street art, and hidden viewpoints like Miradouro da Senhora do Monte.
2. **Challenges**:
    - **Hilly Terrain**: Lisbon is famously built on seven hills, meaning steep inclines and stairs are common.
    - **Cobblestone Streets**: The traditional calçada portuguesa (Portuguese pavement) can be slippery, especially after rain.

Tips for Walking in Lisbon:

- Wear comfortable, sturdy shoes with good grip.
- Take breaks at scenic viewpoints (miradouros) to rest and enjoy the views.
- Avoid heavy walking tours during the midday heat in summer.

Porto

1. **Why Walk in Porto?**
   - Porto's compact city center makes it easy to explore landmarks like the Ribeira district, Livraria Lello, and Clérigos Tower on foot.
   - Walking along the Douro River provides breathtaking views and access to restaurants and bars.
2. **Challenges**:
   - **Hills and Stairs**: Like Lisbon, Porto is hilly, especially around the Ribeira and Gaia areas.
   - **Uneven Streets**: Old cobblestone roads can be tricky to navigate, particularly for those with mobility issues.
3. **Tips for Walking in Porto**:

   - Take the **Luis I Bridge pedestrian walkway** for stunning views while crossing between Porto and Vila Nova de Gaia.
   - Plan shorter walking routes to avoid fatigue, and use public transport for uphill climbs.

Navigating by Bicycle

Lisbon

1. **Cycling in Lisbon:**
   - While Lisbon's hills can be a challenge, the city is increasingly bike-friendly, with dedicated cycling lanes and flat areas ideal for casual rides.
   - **Popular Routes**:
     - Ride along the Tagus River from Cais do Sodré to Belém.
     - Explore the Parque das Nações area, a flat and modern part of the city.

2. **Challenges**:
    - **Hills**: Cycling uphill can be exhausting, so electric bikes are a popular choice.
    - **Traffic**: Be cautious when navigating busy streets, especially during rush hours.
3. **Bike Rentals and Services**:
    - **Gira Bikes**: Lisbon's public bike-sharing system offers affordable rentals, including electric bikes.
    - Private rental shops are available near tourist hubs.

Porto

1. **Cycling in Porto:**
    - Porto is gradually becoming more bike-friendly, with scenic flat routes along the Douro River and beyond.
    - **Popular Routes**:
        - Cycle from Ribeira to Foz do Douro along the river for stunning views.
        - Cross the Luis I Bridge and explore the Gaia waterfront, home to the famous port wine cellars.
2. **Challenges**:
    - **Hills**: Like Lisbon, Porto's steep streets are a challenge for cyclists. Electric bikes are recommended.
    - **Traffic and Narrow Streets**: Old streets can be tricky for cycling, so stick to designated bike paths when possible.
3. **Bike Rentals and Services**:
    - Porto has numerous bike rental shops offering traditional and electric bicycles.
    - Guided cycling tours are available for those who want a structured experience.

Pros and Cons of Navigating by Foot and Bicycle

Mode	Pros	Cons
Walking	- Free and immersive- Access to narrow streets- Great for sightseeing	- Fatigue from hills- Cobblestones can be tough on feet
Cycling	- Covers more ground quickly- Scenic routes along rivers- Environmentally friendly	- Challenging terrain in hilly areas- Traffic and narrow streets in city centers

Tips for Exploring on Foot and by Bicycle

1. **Footwear**: Wear supportive shoes for walking and cycling.
2. **Stay Hydrated**: Especially in summer, keep water handy.
3. **Safety Gear**: Wear a helmet when cycling and use reflective gear at night.
4. **Plan Your Route**: Use maps or apps like Google Maps or Komoot for cycling-friendly routes.
5. **Mix and Match**: Combine walking or cycling with public transportation for longer distances or to avoid steep climbs.

Exploring Lisbon and Porto on foot or by bicycle is a rewarding experience, offering unique perspectives and access to hidden gems. Whether you're strolling through Alfama's winding streets or cycling along Porto's riverside, these modes of travel allow you to truly connect with the cities.

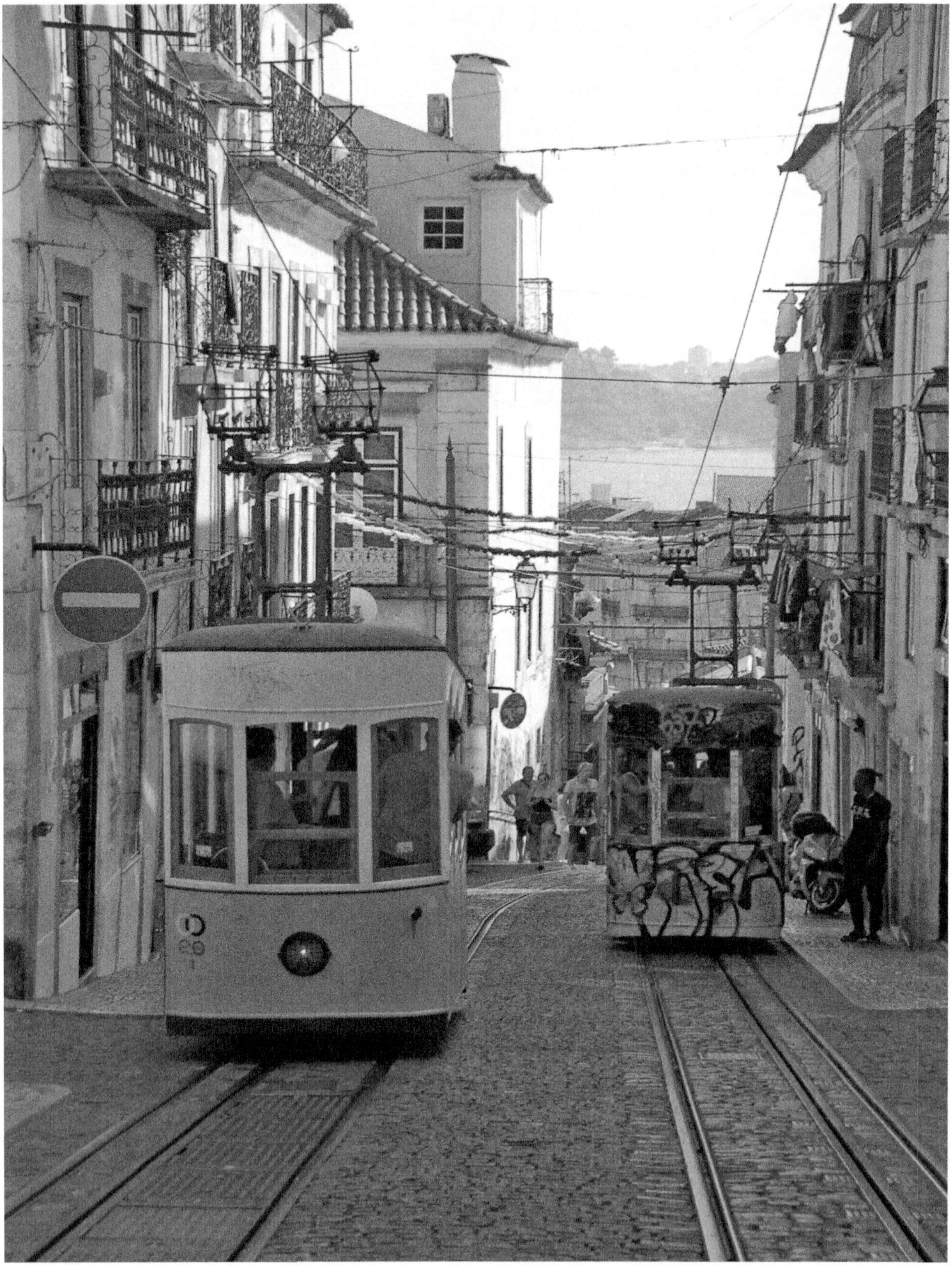

Chapter 4: Accommodation Options

Top Hotels and Boutique Stays in Porto

Porto is home to a variety of exceptional accommodations, offering something for every traveler. From luxurious riverside hotels to cozy boutique stays, these options combine comfort with great locations and outstanding service. Below is a detailed list with highlights, approximate prices, and contact information.

1. The Yeatman

- **Category**: Luxury
- **Highlights**:
    - Panoramic views of the Douro River and Porto's skyline.
    - Michelin-starred restaurant offering exquisite cuisine.
    - Lavish spa with wine-based treatments.
    - Outdoor infinity pool overlooking the city.
- **Approximate Price**: €350–€600 per night.
- **Contact Number**: +351 220 133 100
- **Email**: reservations@theyeatman.com
- **Website**: www.theyeatman.com
- **Address**: Rua do Choupelo, 4400-088 Vila Nova de Gaia, Porto

2. InterContinental Porto - Palácio das Cardosas

- **Category**: Luxury
- **Highlights**:
    - Situated in a restored 18th-century palace.
    - Spacious rooms with luxurious furnishings.
    - Prime location near Avenida dos Aliados and major attractions like Clérigos Tower.
    - Elegant bar and fine dining restaurant.
- **Approximate Price**: €250–€400 per night.
- **Contact Number**: +351 220 035 600
- **Email**: reservations.porto@ihg.com

- **Website**: www.ihg.com
- **Address**: Praça da Liberdade 25, 4000-322 Porto

3. Torel Avantgarde

- **Category**: Boutique Luxury
- **Highlights**:
    - Art-inspired design with unique, themed rooms.
    - Rooftop bar with stunning views of the Douro River.
    - On-site restaurant serving creative Portuguese cuisine.
    - Luxurious spa facilities.
- **Approximate Price**: €180–€300 per night.
- **Contact Number**: +351 220 110 082
- **Email**: reservations@torelavantgarde.com
- **Website**: www.torelavantgarde.com
- **Address**: Rua da Restauração 336, 4050-501 Porto

4. Hotel Infante Sagres

- **Category**: Boutique Luxury
- **Highlights**:
    - Porto's oldest five-star hotel with timeless elegance.
    - Lavish interiors with handcrafted details.
    - On-site restaurant and bar serving gourmet cuisine.
    - Central location near Rua das Flores and Livraria Lello.
- **Approximate Price**: €200–€350 per night.
- **Contact Number**: +351 223 398 500
- **Email**: info@hotelinfantesagres.pt
- **Website**: www.hotelinfantesagres.pt
- **Address**: Praça Filipa de Lencastre 62, 4050-259 Porto

5. Pestana Vintage Porto Hotel & World Heritage Site

- **Category**: Luxury
- **Highlights**:
    - Located in Ribeira, a UNESCO World Heritage area.
    - Stunning views of the Douro River and Luís I Bridge.
    - Luxurious rooms blending modern amenities with historical charm.
    - Excellent riverside restaurant.
- **Approximate Price**: €230–€400 per night.
- **Contact Number**: +351 223 402 300
- **Email**: reservations@pestana.com
- **Website**: www.pestana.com
- **Address**: Praça da Ribeira 1, 4050-513 Porto

---

6. Mo House

- **Category**: Boutique Stay
- **Highlights**:
    - Intimate boutique guesthouse with stylish, minimalist design.
    - Located in the heart of Porto near Ribeira.
    - Personalized service and cozy atmosphere.
    - Complimentary breakfast with local ingredients.
- **Approximate Price**: €100–€180 per night.
- **Contact Number**: +351 915 504 504
- **Email**: hello@mohouseporto.com
- **Website**: www.mohouseporto.com
- **Address**: Rua de São João 50, 4050-552 Porto

---

7. Flores Village Hotel & Spa

- **Category**: Boutique Spa Hotel
- **Highlights**:
    - Located on the picturesque Rua das Flores.
    - Features a spa with sauna, Turkish bath, and indoor pool.
    - Combination of modern design and historical elements.
    - Offers family-friendly apartments and suites.

- **Approximate Price**: €120–€220 per night.
- **Contact Number**: +351 222 013 478
- **Email**: info@floresvillage.com
- **Website**: www.floresvillage.com
- **Address**: Rua das Flores 139, 4050-266 Porto

Tips for Choosing Your Stay in Porto

1. **For Luxury and River Views**: Opt for The Yeatman or Pestana Vintage Porto.
2. **For Central Location**: Choose InterContinental Porto or Hotel Infante Sagres.
3. **For Boutique Charm**: Torel Avantgarde or Mo House are excellent picks.
4. **For Spa Facilities**: Flores Village Hotel & Spa offers a relaxing retreat.

Booking in advance is recommended, especially during peak travel seasons, as these popular hotels tend to fill up quickly!

Accomodations in Porto

Top Hotels and Boutique Stays in Lisbon

Lisbon's hospitality scene offers a diverse range of accommodations, from luxury hotels in historic buildings to chic boutique stays with local charm. Whether you're seeking sophistication, comfort, or a unique experience, Lisbon has something for every traveler. Below is a curated list of the top hotels and boutique stays, complete with highlights, approximate prices, and contact details.

1. Four Seasons Hotel Ritz Lisbon

- **Category**: Luxury
- **Highlights**:
    - Iconic five-star hotel offering panoramic views of Lisbon.
    - Rooftop running track and spa with a heated indoor pool.
    - Elegant rooms featuring classic and modern design elements.
    - Fine dining at CURA, a Michelin-starred restaurant.
- **Approximate Price**: €700–€1,200 per night.
- **Contact Number**: +351 213 811 400
- **Email**: reservations.lisbon@fourseasons.com
- **Website**: www.fourseasons.com/lisbon
- **Address**: Rua Rodrigo da Fonseca 88, 1099-039 Lisbon

2. Bairro Alto Hotel

- **Category**: Boutique Luxury
- **Highlights**:
    - Located in the heart of Lisbon's trendy Bairro Alto district.
    - Rooftop terrace with stunning city and river views.
    - Stylish rooms blending classic and contemporary design.
    - On-site restaurant showcasing Portuguese cuisine.
- **Approximate Price**: €400–€700 per night.
- **Contact Number**: +351 213 408 288
- **Email**: info@bairroaltohotel.com
- **Website**: www.bairroaltohotel.com
- **Address**: Praça Luís de Camões 2, 1200-243 Lisbon

3. Hotel Avenida Palace

- **Category**: Classic Luxury
- **Highlights**:
  - Iconic 19th-century hotel with opulent interiors.
  - Prime location near Rossio Square and Avenida da Liberdade.
  - Exceptional service and old-world charm.
  - Elegant bar with live piano music.
- **Approximate Price**: €250–€500 per night.
- **Contact Number**: +351 213 218 100
- **Email**: info@hotelavenidapalace.pt
- **Website**: www.hotelavenidapalace.pt
- **Address**: Rua 1º de Dezembro 123, 1200-359 Lisbon

---

4. Memmo Alfama Hotel

- **Category**: Boutique Stay
- **Highlights**:
  - Located in the charming Alfama district, surrounded by historic streets and Fado music.
  - Rooftop terrace with an infinity pool and river views.
  - Modern minimalist design with an emphasis on comfort.
  - Complimentary walking tours of Alfama for guests.
- **Approximate Price**: €200–€400 per night.
- **Contact Number**: +351 210 495 660
- **Email**: reservations.alfama@memmohotels.com
- **Website**: www.memmohotels.com
- **Address**: Travessa das Merceeiras 27, 1100-348 Lisbon

---

5. The Lumiares Hotel & Spa

- **Category**: Boutique Apartment Hotel
- **Highlights**:
  - Stylish apartment-style rooms with fully equipped kitchens.
  - Rooftop restaurant and bar with panoramic views of Lisbon.
  - On-site spa offering a range of treatments.

- ○ Located in Bairro Alto, ideal for nightlife and shopping.
- **Approximate Price**: €250–€450 per night.
- **Contact Number**: +351 211 160 200
- **Email**: reservations@thelumiares.com
- **Website**: www.thelumiares.com
- **Address**: Rua do Diário de Notícias 142, 1200-146 Lisbon

---

6. Santiago de Alfama - Boutique Hotel

- **Category**: Boutique Stay
- **Highlights**:
  - ○ Nestled in a historic building in Alfama, Lisbon's oldest district.
  - ○ Luxuriously designed rooms with a cozy, home-like feel.
  - ○ On-site restaurant serving local and international cuisine.
  - ○ Excellent service with a personal touch.
- **Approximate Price**: €300–€500 per night.
- **Contact Number**: +351 213 941 616
- **Email**: reservations@santiagodealfama.com
- **Website**: www.santiagodealfama.com
- **Address**: Rua de Santiago 10, 1100-494 Lisbon

---

7. Corpo Santo Lisbon Historical Hotel

- **Category**: Boutique Luxury
- **Highlights**:
  - ○ Located in a historic area near Cais do Sodré and the riverfront.
  - ○ Unique design incorporating original 17th-century walls.
  - ○ Complimentary tours of Lisbon's historic districts.
  - ○ Free snacks and drinks in the lobby for guests.
- **Approximate Price**: €200–€400 per night.
- **Contact Number**: +351 218 288 000
- **Email**: reservations@corposantohotel.com
- **Website**: www.corposantohotel.com
- **Address**: Largo do Corpo Santo 25, 1200-129 Lisbon

8. My Story Hotel Ouro

- **Category**: Mid-Range Boutique Stay
- **Highlights**:
    - Charming hotel with vintage-inspired interiors.
    - Centrally located in Baixa, close to major attractions.
    - Friendly service and good value for money.
    - On-site café serving delicious breakfast and snacks.
- **Approximate Price**: €120–€250 per night.
- **Contact Number**: +351 213 400 340
- **Email**: ouro@mystoryhotels.com
- **Website**: www.mystoryhotels.com
- **Address**: Rua Áurea 100, 1100-063 Lisbon

Tips for Choosing Your Stay in Lisbon

1. **For Luxury and Amenities**: Choose Four Seasons Hotel Ritz Lisbon or Bairro Alto Hotel.
2. **For Central Locations**: Hotel Avenida Palace or Corpo Santo Lisbon Historical Hotel are excellent picks.
3. **For Boutique Charm**: Memmo Alfama or Santiago de Alfama offer intimate, unique stays.
4. **For Apartment-Style Comfort**: The Lumiares Hotel & Spa is a top choice.

With its wide variety of accommodations, Lisbon ensures a memorable stay for every type of traveler. Book early, especially in peak travel months, to secure your ideal spot!

Accomodations in Lisbon

Budget-Friendly Hostels in Porto

Porto is a fantastic destination for travelers on a budget, offering many affordable and comfortable hostel options. Whether you're a solo traveler looking to meet new friends or simply seeking wallet-friendly accommodations, these hostels provide excellent amenities and prime locations without breaking the bank. Here's a curated list with highlights, approximate prices, and contact details.

1. The House of Sandeman - Hostel & Suites

- **Category**: Boutique Hostel
- **Highlights**:
  - Unique wine-themed hostel located in Vila Nova de Gaia.
  - Stylish dorms and private suites with stunning views of the Douro River.
  - Free walking tours and activities organized by the hostel.
  - On-site restaurant and bar serving local delicacies and Sandeman Port wine.
- **Approximate Price**: €25–€60 per night.
- **Contact Number**: +351 220 965 302
- **Email**: info@houseofsandeman.pt
- **Website**: www.houseofsandeman.pt
- **Address**: Largo Miguel Bombarda 3, 4400-222 Vila Nova de Gaia, Porto

---

2. Gallery Hostel

- **Category**: Boutique Hostel
- **Highlights**:
  - Stylish design combining modern and traditional Portuguese elements.
  - Dorms and private rooms with comfortable beds and en-suite bathrooms.
  - On-site art gallery showcasing local artists.
  - Delicious homemade breakfasts included in the price.
- **Approximate Price**: €20–€50 per night.
- **Contact Number**: +351 224 964 313
- **Email**: info@gallery-hostel.com
- **Website**: www.gallery-hostel.com
- **Address**: Rua Miguel Bombarda 222, 4050-377 Porto

3. Yes! Porto Hostel

- **Category**: Party-Friendly Hostel
- **Highlights**:
  - Fun, sociable atmosphere with organized pub crawls and activities.
  - Central location near São Bento Station and Ribeira.
  - Modern facilities, including a well-equipped kitchen and cozy common areas.
  - Free walking tours of Porto for guests.
- **Approximate Price**: €18–€35 per night.
- **Contact Number**: +351 919 173 824
- **Email**: porto@yeshostels.com
- **Website**: www.yeshostels.com
- **Address**: Rua Arquitecto Nicolau Nazoni 31, 4050-423 Porto

---

4. Selina Porto

- **Category**: Trendy Hostel
- **Highlights**:
  - Stylish, Instagram-worthy design with bohemian vibes.
  - Variety of accommodations, including dorms, private rooms, and suites.
  - Co-working spaces, yoga classes, and a vibrant café on-site.
  - Located in Cedofeita, a lively and artsy neighborhood.
- **Approximate Price**: €25–€60 per night.
- **Contact Number**: +351 220 167 784
- **Email**: selina.porto@selina.com
- **Website**: www.selina.com
- **Address**: Rua das Oliveiras 61, 4050-449 Porto

---

5. Porto Spot Hostel

- **Category**: Classic Hostel
- **Highlights**:
  - Great atmosphere for meeting other travelers.
  - Comfortable dorms and private rooms with modern amenities.
  - Spacious common areas and an outdoor terrace.

- o Affordable dinners and pub crawls organized by the hostel.
- **Approximate Price**: €17–€40 per night.
- **Contact Number**: +351 936 103 931
- **Email**: info@portospothostel.com
- **Website**: www.portospothostel.com
- **Address**: Rua Gonçalo Cristóvão 12, 4000-263 Porto

---

6. Nice Way Porto Hostel

- **Category**: Sociable Hostel
- **Highlights**:
  - o Central location near Clérigos Tower and Livraria Lello.
  - o Friendly staff and a welcoming atmosphere.
  - o Organized dinners and group activities.
  - o Clean, modern dorms and private rooms.
- **Approximate Price**: €19–€45 per night.
- **Contact Number**: +351 932 058 439
- **Email**: porto@nicewayhostels.com
- **Website**: www.nicewayhostels.com
- **Address**: Rua Sampaio Bruno 12, 4000-439 Porto

---

7. Rivoli Cinema Hostel

- **Category**: Themed Hostel
- **Highlights**:
  - o Movie-themed hostel with rooms inspired by iconic films.
  - o Rooftop terrace with views of Porto's skyline.
  - o Game room, movie nights, and karaoke events.
  - o Central location near Bolhão Market and Aliados Avenue.
- **Approximate Price**: €16–€35 per night.
- **Contact Number**: +351 223 203 768
- **Email**: info@rivieracinemahostel.com
- **Website**: www.rivieracinemahostel.com
- **Address**: Rua Dr. Magalhães Lemos 83, 4000-332 Porto

Tips for Staying in Porto on a Budget

1. **Book Early**: Popular hostels tend to fill up quickly, especially in summer.
2. **Check Amenities**: Many hostels offer free walking tours, breakfasts, or events, adding value to your stay.
3. **Location Matters**: Choose a hostel close to your main points of interest to save on transportation costs.

Porto's hostels offer a warm, budget-friendly welcome to travelers from all over the world. Enjoy your stay!

Budget-Friendly Hostels in Lisbon

Lisbon is a haven for budget-conscious travelers, offering an excellent selection of hostels that combine affordability, comfort, and a sociable atmosphere. Whether you're a backpacker or simply looking for affordable lodging, these hostels provide great amenities, prime locations, and a chance to meet fellow travelers. Here's a list of some of the best budget-friendly hostels in Lisbon, with highlights, approximate prices, and contact details.

1. Home Lisbon Hostel

- **Category**: Award-Winning Hostel
- **Highlights**:
    - Famous for "Mamma's Dinners," homemade meals prepared by the hostel owner's mom.
    - Central location in Baixa, near major attractions like Rossio Square.
    - Spacious dorms with individual lockers and reading lights.
    - Friendly atmosphere with free walking tours and pub crawls.
- **Approximate Price**: €20–€40 per night.
- **Contact Number**: +351 218 885 312
- **Email**: info@homelisbonhostel.com
- **Website**: www.homelisbonhostel.com
- **Address**: Rua de São Nicolau 13, 1100-547 Lisbon

2. Lisbon Destination Hostel

- **Category**: Designer Hostel
- **Highlights**:
  - Located inside the iconic Rossio Train Station.
  - Beautifully designed dorms and private rooms with modern amenities.
  - Indoor garden lounge and entertainment areas.
  - Daily events like walking tours, wine tastings, and movie nights.
- **Approximate Price**: €18–€35 per night.
- **Contact Number**: +351 210 115 922
- **Email**: info@lisbondestinationhostel.com
- **Website**: www.destinationhostels.com
- **Address**: Rossio Train Station, 2nd Floor, Praça dos Restauradores, 1249-970 Lisbon

---

3. Yes! Lisbon Hostel

- **Category**: Party-Friendly Hostel
- **Highlights**:
  - Vibrant atmosphere with nightly pub crawls and communal dinners.
  - Central location near Praça do Comércio and Baixa-Chiado.
  - Comfortable beds with individual curtains, lights, and outlets.
  - Free walking tours and social activities for guests.
- **Approximate Price**: €19–€35 per night.
- **Contact Number**: +351 936 190 534
- **Email**: lisbon@yeshostels.com
- **Website**: www.yeshostels.com
- **Address**: Rua de São Julião 148, 1100-527 Lisbon

---

4. Selina Secret Garden Lisbon

- **Category**: Trendy Hostel
- **Highlights**:
  - Modern and stylish hostel with co-working spaces and a rooftop pool.
  - Variety of room options, including dorms, private rooms, and suites.
  - On-site restaurant, café, and wellness activities like yoga.

    - Located in Cais do Sodré, close to nightlife and the riverfront.
- **Approximate Price**: €25–€60 per night.
- **Contact Number**: +351 211 664 591
- **Email**: lisbon.secretgarden@selina.com
- **Website**: www.selina.com
- **Address**: Beco Carrasco 1, 1200-096 Lisbon

---

5. Goodmorning Solo Traveller Hostel

- **Category**: Sociable Hostel
- **Highlights**:
    - Specifically designed for solo travelers, fostering a friendly atmosphere.
    - Central location near Restauradores Square and Avenida da Liberdade.
    - Free daily breakfast with homemade waffles.
    - Evening events like sangria nights and cooking classes.
- **Approximate Price**: €22–€40 per night.
- **Contact Number**: +351 213 421 128
- **Email**: info@goodmorninghostel.com
- **Website**: www.goodmorninghostel.com
- **Address**: Praça dos Restauradores 65, 1250-188 Lisbon

---

6. Sunset Destination Hostel

- **Category**: Rooftop Vibes
- **Highlights**:
    - Stunning rooftop terrace with a pool overlooking the Tagus River.
    - Located inside Cais do Sodré Train Station.
    - Comfortable dorms and private rooms with modern amenities.
    - Free walking tours and sunset parties.
- **Approximate Price**: €18–€35 per night.
- **Contact Number**: +351 213 461 381
- **Email**: info@sunsetdestinationhostel.com
- **Website**: www.destinationhostels.com
- **Address**: Cais do Sodré Train Station, 1st Floor, Praça Duque da Terceira, 1200-161 Lisbon

7. Lost Inn Lisbon Hostel

- **Category**: Classic Hostel
- **Highlights**:
    - Spacious and clean dorms with large windows and natural light.
    - Free walking tours and nightly sangria sessions.
    - Prime location near Chiado and Bairro Alto.
    - Welcoming and helpful staff.
- **Approximate Price**: €18–€30 per night.
- **Contact Number**: +351 213 470 690
- **Email**: info@lostinnlisbon.com
- **Website**: www.lostinnlisbon.com
- **Address**: Rua de São Nicolau 120, 1100-549 Lisbon

---

8. HUB New Lisbon Hostel

- **Category**: Youthful and Fun
- **Highlights**:
    - Features a ball pit in the lounge area for fun and relaxation.
    - Located in Bairro Alto, ideal for exploring Lisbon's nightlife.
    - Affordable dorms and private rooms with colorful decor.
    - Terrace with hammocks and a small pool.
- **Approximate Price**: €15–€30 per night.
- **Contact Number**: +351 211 976 724
- **Email**: info@hubhostel.com
- **Website**: www.hubhostel.com
- **Address**: Rua de O Século 150, 1200-437 Lisbon

Tips for Staying in Lisbon on a Budget

1. **Plan Ahead**: Book hostels early, especially during peak travel seasons.
2. **Check Perks**: Many hostels offer free breakfasts, walking tours, and social activities.
3. **Location is Key**: Staying in central neighborhoods like Baixa, Chiado, or Bairro Alto saves on transportation costs.

With its variety of affordable and high-quality hostels, Lisbon ensures budget travelers can enjoy the city in comfort and style.

Family and Group-Friendly Rentals

Portugal's charm is best enjoyed with loved ones, and both Porto and Lisbon offer a variety of family- and group-friendly rentals that cater to larger groups, ensuring comfort, privacy, and an authentic local experience. These accommodations typically feature spacious layouts, fully equipped kitchens, and convenient locations, making them ideal for families or groups traveling together. Below are some top options in both cities, including highlights, approximate prices, and contact details.

Porto: Family and Group-Friendly Rentals

1. Feel Porto Downtown Townhouses

- **Highlights**:
    - Luxurious apartments in the heart of Porto, ideal for families or groups.
    - Fully equipped kitchens, spacious living areas, and multiple bedrooms.
    - Concierge services available for tours, airport transfers, and babysitting.
- **Approximate Price**: €150–€300 per night (for 4–8 guests).
- **Contact Number**: +351 965 698 096
- **Email**: info@feelporto.com
- **Website**: www.feelporto.com
- **Address**: Rua Guedes de Azevedo 131, 4000-111 Porto

2. Ribeira Apartments

- **Highlights**:
    - Stunning riverfront apartments in Porto's historic Ribeira district.
    - Spacious units with modern amenities and gorgeous views of the Douro River.
    - Walking distance to Porto's main attractions like Dom Luís I Bridge.
- **Approximate Price**: €120–€250 per night (for 4–6 guests).
- **Contact Number**: +351 918 870 553
- **Email**: info@ribeiraapartments.com
- **Website**: www.ribeiraapartments.com
- **Address**: Rua do Infante D. Henrique 26, 4050-296 Porto

3. Oporto Loft Apartments

- **Highlights**:
    - Modern apartments with a mix of contemporary and rustic Portuguese decor.
    - Ideal for families, offering amenities like cribs, high chairs, and laundry facilities.
    - Located in Cedofeita, a quiet area with easy access to downtown Porto.
- **Approximate Price**: €100–€200 per night (for 4–6 guests).
- **Contact Number**: +351 914 312 576
- **Email**: bookings@oportoloft.com
- **Website**: www.oportoloft.com
- **Address**: Rua da Boavista 703, 4050-110 Porto

Lisbon: Family and Group-Friendly Rentals

1. Lisbon Five Stars Apartments - São Paulo 55

- **Highlights**:
    - Stylish, fully furnished apartments with high ceilings and elegant decor.
    - Centrally located near Cais do Sodré, perfect for exploring Lisbon.
    - Multiple-bedroom units accommodate families and larger groups.
- **Approximate Price**: €150–€400 per night (for 6–10 guests).
- **Contact Number**: +351 927 531 896
- **Email**: reservations@lisbonfivestars.pt
- **Website**: www.lisbonfivestars.pt
- **Address**: Rua de São Paulo 55, 1200-018 Lisbon

2. Altido Downtown Deluxe Apartments

- **Highlights**:
    - Large, modern apartments in Lisbon's downtown area.
    - Well-equipped kitchens, spacious living areas, and family-friendly features.
    - Walking distance to Praça do Comércio and Rossio Square.
- **Approximate Price**: €130–€300 per night (for 4–8 guests).
- **Contact Number**: +351 910 123 456
- **Email**: bookings@stayaltido.com
- **Website**: www.altido.com

- **Address**: Rua da Madalena 67, 1100-318 Lisbon

3. Martinhal Lisbon Chiado Family Suites

- Highlights:
    - Designed specifically for families, with kid-friendly amenities like play areas and babysitting services.
    - Luxurious suites featuring full kitchens and modern interiors.
    - Located in the heart of Chiado, near shops, restaurants, and cultural landmarks.
- **Approximate Price**: €200–€400 per night (for 4–6 guests).
- **Contact Number**: +351 210 515 200
- **Email**: chiado@martinhal.com
- **Website**: www.martinhal.com
- **Address**: Rua das Flores 44, 1200-195 Lisbon

4. Alfama Yellow House

- Highlights:
    - Cozy townhouse located in the historic Alfama district.
    - Ideal for families seeking a traditional Portuguese neighborhood vibe.
    - Fully equipped with kitchen, laundry facilities, and multiple bedrooms.
- **Approximate Price**: €100–€200 per night (for 4–6 guests).
- **Contact Number**: +351 918 123 789
- **Email**: bookings@alfamayellow.com
- **Website**: N/A
- **Address**: Rua da Regueira 35, 1100-435 Lisbon

Tips for Family and Group Rentals

1. **Book in Advance**: Larger accommodations can be in high demand, especially during peak seasons.
2. **Look for Kid-Friendly Amenities**: Cribs, high chairs, and laundry facilities can make your stay easier.
3. **Check for Accessibility**: If you're traveling with elderly family members or strollers, ensure the property has elevators or is on the ground floor.
4. **Proximity to Attractions**: Choose a rental close to public transport or within walking distance of major sights to save time and energy.

Chapter 5: Cultural Insights

Language Basics and Useful Phrases

Language Basics and 100 Useful Phrases for Traveling in Portugal

Portuguese is the official language of Portugal, and while many locals in Lisbon and Porto speak English, learning some basic phrases can go a long way in enhancing your travel experience. Knowing a few words can help you navigate more easily, show respect for the local culture, and even create deeper connections with the people you meet.

Portuguese Language Basics

Portuguese pronunciation can be tricky, so here are a few tips:

- **Vowels**:
    - "A" sounds like *ah* as in "father."
    - "E" sounds like *eh* (like "met") or *ee* (like "see").
    - "O" sounds like *oo* (like "book") or *oh* (like "go").
    - "U" sounds like *oo* as in "moon."
- **Common Sounds**:
    - "R" is pronounced like a guttural "H" in some regions (e.g., "Rio" sounds like "Hee-oo").
    - "Ç" (cedilla) is pronounced as "s" (e.g., "faça" sounds like "fah-sah").
- **Key Politeness Words**:
    - Please: *Por favor*
    - Thank you: *Obrigado* (male speakers) / *Obrigada* (female speakers)
    - Excuse me: *Com licença*
    - Sorry: *Desculpe*

100 Useful Portuguese Phrases

Basic Greetings

1. Hello: *Olá*
2. Good morning: *Bom dia*
3. Good afternoon: *Boa tarde*
4. Good evening/night: *Boa noite*
5. How are you?: *Como está?*
6. I'm fine, thank you: *Estou bem, obrigado/obrigada*
7. Nice to meet you: *Prazer em conhecê-lo/conhecê-la*

Polite Expressions

8. Please: *Por favor*
9. Thank you: *Obrigado/Obrigada*
10. You're welcome: *De nada*
11. Excuse me: *Com licença*
12. Sorry: *Desculpe*
13. No problem: *Sem problema*

Travel Essentials

14. Where is the airport?: *Onde fica o aeroporto?*
15. Where is the train station?: *Onde fica a estação de trem?*
16. How much is a ticket?: *Quanto custa um bilhete?*
17. What time is the train/bus?: *A que horas é o trem/autocarro?*
18. Can you help me?: *Pode ajudar-me?*
19. I'm lost: *Estou perdido/perdida*
20. I need a taxi: *Preciso de um táxi*

Dining and Food

21. I would like…: *Eu gostaria de…*
22. Can I see the menu?: *Posso ver o menu?*
23. A table for two, please: *Uma mesa para dois, por favor*
24. Water, please: *Água, por favor*

25. Wine, please: *Vinho, por favor*
26. The bill, please: *A conta, por favor*
27. Is this dish vegetarian?: *Este prato é vegetariano?*
28. Cheers!: *Saúde!*

Shopping

29. How much does this cost?: *Quanto custa isso?*
30. Do you accept credit cards?: *Aceita cartões de crédito?*
31. Can I have a receipt?: *Posso ter um recibo?*
32. I'm just looking: *Estou só a ver*
33. Do you have this in another size/color?: *Tem isto noutra cor/tamanho?*

Directions

34. Where is the restroom?: *Onde fica a casa de banho?*
35. Left: *Esquerda*
36. Right: *Direita*
37. Straight ahead: *Em frente*
38. Near: *Perto*
39. Far: *Longe*

Emergency Phrases

40. Help!: *Ajuda!*
41. Call the police: *Chame a polícia*
42. I need a doctor: *Preciso de um médico*
43. I'm sick: *Estou doente*
44. My phone is lost: *Perdi o meu telemóvel*

Numbers and Time

45. One: *Um*
46. Two: *Dois/Duas*
47. Three: *Três*
48. Four: *Quatro*

49. Five: *Cinco*
50. Ten: *Dez*
51. What time is it?: *Que horas são?*
52. Morning: *Manhã*
53. Afternoon: *Tarde*
54. Evening/Night: *Noite*

Social Interactions

55. Can you speak English?: *Fala inglês?*
56. I don't understand: *Não entendo*
57. Can you repeat that?: *Pode repetir isso?*
58. Yes: *Sim*
59. No: *Não*
60. Maybe: *Talvez*
61. I like it: *Eu gosto*
62. I don't like it: *Eu não gosto*
63. I'm happy: *Estou feliz*
64. I'm tired: *Estou cansado/cansada*

Transportation

65. Where can I buy a ticket?: *Onde posso comprar um bilhete?*
66. Is it far?: *É longe?*
67. How long does it take?: *Quanto tempo demora?*
68. Which bus/train should I take?: *Qual autocarro/trem devo apanhar?*

Accommodation

69. I have a reservation: *Tenho uma reserva*
70. Do you have a room available?: *Tem um quarto disponível?*
71. What's the price per night?: *Qual é o preço por noite?*
72. Can I check out later?: *Posso fazer o check-out mais tarde?*

Bonus Tips for Speaking Portuguese

1. **Practice Pronunciation**: Listen to locals and mimic their speech patterns.
2. **Use a Translation App**: Google Translate or other apps can help with difficult words.
3. **Be Patient**: Most Portuguese speakers appreciate your effort to speak their language, even if you make mistakes.

Learning these phrases will help you navigate Porto and Lisbon with confidence while making your trip smoother and more enjoyable. Practice these basics before your trip, and you'll be ready to explore Portugal like a local!

Customs and Etiquette in Portugal

Understanding local customs and etiquette is an essential part of respectful and enjoyable travel. Portugal has a rich cultural heritage, and its people are known for their warmth and hospitality. By following a few simple guidelines, you can show respect for Portuguese traditions and blend in more seamlessly during your visit to Lisbon, Porto, or other parts of the country.

Greetings and Politeness

- **Greetings**: A handshake is the standard way to greet someone, whether in a formal or casual setting. Among friends or family, women often exchange cheek kisses—typically two, starting with the right cheek—while men might embrace or pat each other on the back.
- **Titles and Formality**: Address people with titles like *Senhor* (Mr.) or *Senhora* (Mrs.) followed by their last name, especially in formal settings. First names are used once a closer relationship is established.
- **Politeness**: Portuguese people value good manners. Always say *por favor* (please), *obrigado/obrigada* (thank you), and *com licença* (excuse me).

Dining Etiquette

- **Timing**: Lunch is typically from 12:30 PM to 2:30 PM, and dinner starts late, often after 8:00 PM. Dining out later in the evening is common, especially in Lisbon and Porto.
- **Table Manners**:
    - Wait to be seated by your host.
    - Keep your hands visible on the table but avoid resting your elbows.
    - Eating slowly is appreciated, as meals are meant to be enjoyed.
- **Sharing Food**: Sharing dishes, especially starters, is common. If bread, olives, or cheese are brought to the table, they are not complimentary unless explicitly stated on the menu.
- **Tipping**: Tipping is appreciated but not mandatory. A 5–10% tip is considered generous for good service.

Social Behavior

- **Personal Space**: Portuguese people are comfortable with close physical proximity during conversations. Don't be surprised by light touches on the arm or shoulder.
- **Punctuality**: While punctuality is appreciated for business meetings, social gatherings tend to be more relaxed. Being a few minutes late is usually acceptable.
- **Small Talk**: Portuguese people enjoy talking about food, wine, football (soccer), and family. Avoid controversial topics such as politics unless you know someone well.

Cultural Norms

- **Family**: Family is central to Portuguese culture. You might notice large family gatherings at restaurants or public events.
- **Religion**: Portugal is predominantly Roman Catholic, and religious traditions are an integral part of life. Respect for churches and religious customs is expected; dress modestly when visiting religious sites.
- **Festivals**: Local festivals, such as *Festas dos Santos Populares* (celebrated in June), are lively and communal. Participating respectfully is encouraged!

Dress Code

- **Casual but Neat**: In urban areas like Lisbon and Porto, people tend to dress stylishly but not overly formal.
- **Religious Sites**: Avoid wearing revealing clothing when visiting churches or monasteries.
- **Beachwear**: Beach attire is acceptable on the beach but not in city streets or restaurants.

Transportation Etiquette

- **Public Transportation**: Always offer your seat to the elderly, pregnant women, or those with small children. Queue politely at bus or tram stops.
- **Taxis and Ride-Sharing**: A small tip (around 5–10%) is appreciated but not expected.

Photography

- **Ask for Permission**: Before photographing people, especially locals, ask for their consent.
- **Religious Sites**: Some churches or monasteries may prohibit photography. Look for signs or ask a guide before taking pictures.

Do's and Don'ts

Do:

- Learn a few basic Portuguese phrases, even if locals speak English.
- Show interest in Portuguese food, wine, and traditions—it's a source of pride for locals.
- Be patient, as the pace of life is more relaxed compared to some other countries.

Don't:

- Criticize Portuguese culture or compare it unfavorably to other countries.
- Assume all Portuguese people are the same—regional differences are significant, especially between the north (e.g., Porto) and the south (e.g., Lisbon).

- Be loud or disruptive in public places; Portuguese culture values calm and respectful behavior.

By understanding and respecting these customs, you'll not only enrich your experience in Portugal but also leave a positive impression on the locals you encounter.

Local Festivals and Events in Porto and Lisbon

Portugal is a country rich in traditions and celebrations, with festivals that reflect its cultural heritage, history, and vibrant community spirit. Porto and Lisbon, two of its most iconic cities, host an array of festivals and events throughout the year, offering visitors a chance to immerse themselves in Portuguese culture, music, cuisine, and customs.

Festivals in Lisbon

1. Festas de Lisboa (Festivals of Lisbon)

- **When**: Entire month of June (peaks on June 12th-13th)
- **Highlights**:
    - Celebrates the city's patron saint, Santo António.
    - Streets are decorated with lights and garlands.
    - Alfama district hosts traditional sardine grilling, folk music, and street parties.
    - The Santo António Wedding tradition includes a mass wedding for couples.
- **Don't Miss**: The parade on Avenida da Liberdade, where neighborhoods compete with elaborate floats and dances.

2. Lisbon Carnival

- **When**: February (dates vary with Lent)
- **Highlights**:
    - Colorful parades with samba-inspired costumes and music.
    - Festivities in the Praça do Comércio and along the Tagus River.
    - A mix of Brazilian and traditional Portuguese carnival vibes.
- **Tip**: Dress up and join the celebrations to feel part of the community.

3. NOS Alive Music Festival

- **When**: July (exact dates vary)
- **Highlights**:
  - One of Europe's top music festivals, held in Algés, just outside Lisbon.
  - Features international rock, indie, and electronic music stars.
  - Attracts thousands of fans from across the globe.
- **Tip**: Book tickets and accommodation early, as the festival draws huge crowds.

4. Christmas in Lisbon

- **When**: December
- **Highlights**:
  - Streets illuminated with festive lights.
  - Christmas markets like Campo Pequeno feature handmade crafts and traditional foods.
  - Choir performances in historic churches.
- **Don't Miss**: The giant Christmas tree in Praça do Comércio.

Festivals in Porto

1. São João Festival (Festival of St. John)

- **When**: June 23rd-24th
- **Highlights**:
  - The most famous festival in Porto, celebrating the city's patron saint.
  - Locals and tourists gather for street parties, live music, and traditional foods.
  - Unique traditions include hitting people with plastic hammers and releasing lanterns.
  - The night ends with a spectacular fireworks display over the Douro River.
- **Tip**: Join a boat cruise on the Douro for the best view of the fireworks.

2. Fantasporto (International Film Festival)

- **When**: February-March (exact dates vary)
- **Highlights**:
  - Celebrates fantasy, sci-fi, and independent cinema.
  - Screenings and events at historic venues like Rivoli Theatre.

- o Perfect for film enthusiasts.
- **Don't Miss**: Networking events and workshops with filmmakers.

3. Porto Wine Fest

- **When**: September (exact dates vary)
- **Highlights**:
    - o Held in Vila Nova de Gaia, across the Douro River.
    - o Showcases Portugal's renowned wines, including port and vinho verde.
    - o Wine tastings, workshops, and food pairings.
- **Tip**: Try the local petiscos (Portuguese tapas) with your wine.

4. Christmas and New Year in Porto

- **When**: December
- **Highlights**:
    - o Christmas markets, including Mercado de Natal in Ribeira.
    - o Illuminated streets and festive decorations, especially around Avenida dos Aliados.
    - o Fireworks and concerts to welcome the New Year.
- **Don't Miss**: Ice skating rinks and holiday treats like bolo rei (king cake).

Cultural Events in Both Cities

1. Fado Nights

- **When**: Year-round
- **Where**: Alfama (Lisbon) and Ribeira (Porto) districts.
- **Highlights**:
    - o Intimate performances of Fado, Portugal's soulful traditional music.
    - o Often accompanied by a meal featuring local cuisine.
- **Tip**: Book in advance for popular Fado houses like Clube de Fado (Lisbon) or Casa da Música (Porto).

2. Portuguese National Day

- **When**: June 10th
- **Highlights**:
  - Celebrations of Portugal's national identity with parades, concerts, and fireworks.
  - Official ceremonies often held in Lisbon, but festivities are nationwide.

Tips for Enjoying Festivals

1. **Plan Ahead**: Popular festivals like São João and Festas de Lisboa attract crowds, so book accommodations and tickets in advance.
2. **Dress Comfortably**: Festivals often involve walking, dancing, or standing, so wear comfortable shoes and clothing.
3. **Join the Locals**: Participate in traditions like grilling sardines or hitting plastic hammers during São João to fully enjoy the experience.
4. **Respect Traditions**: Learn about the cultural significance of events to appreciate them better.

Portugal's festivals and events offer an unforgettable glimpse into its culture and hospitality. Whether you're dancing at a street party or sipping wine by the Douro, the celebrations in Lisbon and Porto promise memories to last a lifetime.

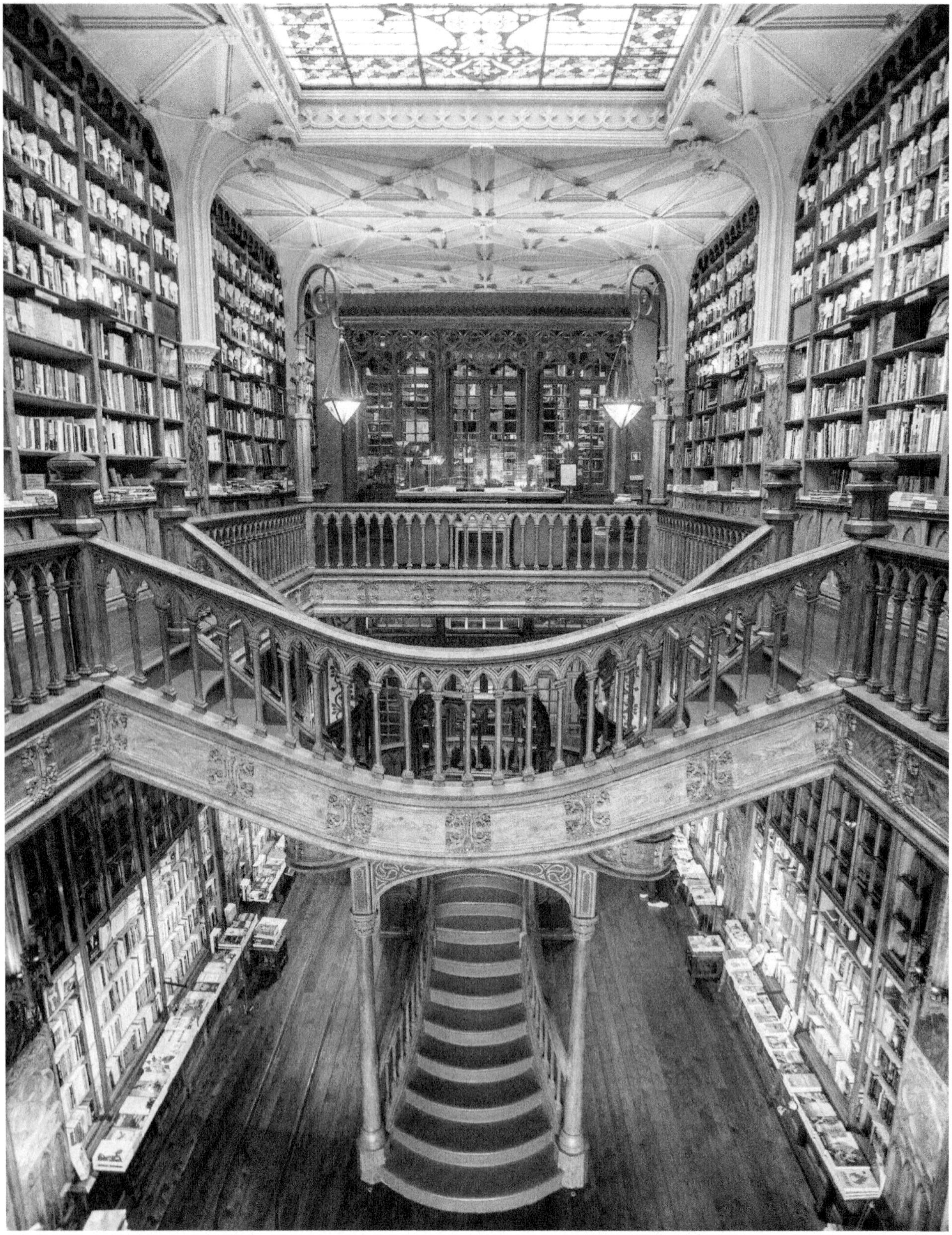

Chapter 6: Porto: The Invincible City

Top Attractions in Porto

Porto is a city filled with captivating sights that blend history, culture, and scenic beauty. Here's a detailed guide to Porto's top attractions, complete with highlights, visiting hours, locations, and entrance fees.

1. Ribeira District (Cais da Ribeira)

- **Highlights**:
    - UNESCO World Heritage Site with colorful houses, cobblestone streets, and riverside dining.
    - Offers spectacular views of the Douro River and the Dom Luís I Bridge.
- **Opening Hours**: Open 24/7.
- **Location**: Ribeira, 4050-505 Porto, Portugal.
- **Fees**: Free to explore.

2. Livraria Lello (Lello Bookstore)

- **Highlights**:
    - Renowned as one of the most beautiful bookstores in the world, featuring neo-Gothic architecture, a grand staircase, and stunning stained glass ceilings.
    - Known for its rumored inspiration to J.K. Rowling's *Harry Potter*.
- **Opening Hours**:
    - Monday to Sunday: 9:30 AM – 7:00 PM.
- **Location**: Rua das Carmelitas 144, 4050-161 Porto, Portugal.
- **Fees**: €5 (ticket redeemable toward book purchases).

3. Dom Luís I Bridge

- **Highlights**:
  - A double-deck iron bridge spanning the Douro River, designed by a student of Gustave Eiffel.
  - Offers panoramic views of Porto and Vila Nova de Gaia.
- **Opening Hours**: Open 24/7.
- **Location**: Pte. Luiz I, 4000-536 Porto, Portugal.
- **Fees**: Free to cross.

---

4. Clerigos Tower (Torre dos Clérigos)

- **Highlights**:
  - A baroque tower with a 360-degree view of the city from the top.
  - Part of the Clérigos Church complex.
- **Opening Hours**:
  - Monday to Sunday: 9:00 AM – 7:00 PM.
- **Location**: Rua de São Filipe de Nery, 4050-546 Porto, Portugal.
- **Fees**: €6 per person.

---

5. Porto Cathedral (Sé do Porto)

- **Highlights**:
  - A 12th-century Romanesque cathedral with gothic cloisters and stunning views of the city.
  - Houses beautiful azulejos (blue and white tiles).
- **Opening Hours**:
  - Monday to Saturday: 9:00 AM – 6:00 PM.
  - Sunday: 9:00 AM – 12:30 PM and 2:30 PM – 6:00 PM.
- **Location**: Terreiro da Sé, 4050-573 Porto, Portugal.
- **Fees**: €3 (includes cloisters).

6. Palácio da Bolsa (Stock Exchange Palace)

- **Highlights**:
    - A 19th-century palace with opulent rooms like the Moorish-inspired Arab Room.
    - Guided tours available to explore its rich history and architecture.
- **Opening Hours**:
    - Monday to Sunday: 9:00 AM – 6:30 PM (summer); 9:00 AM – 12:30 PM and 2:00 PM – 5:30 PM (winter).
- **Location**: Rua Ferreira Borges, 4050-253 Porto, Portugal.
- **Fees**: €10 (guided tour included).

---

7. São Bento Railway Station

- **Highlights**:
    - Famous for its interior decorated with over 20,000 azulejos depicting historical events.
    - A functional train station and a cultural landmark.
- **Opening Hours**: Open 24/7.
- **Location**: Praça Almeida Garrett, 4000-069 Porto, Portugal.
- **Fees**: Free to visit.

---

8. Port Wine Cellars (Caves do Vinho do Porto)

- **Highlights**:
    - Located across the river in Vila Nova de Gaia, these cellars offer guided tours and tastings of the city's famous port wine.
    - Popular cellars include Sandeman, Graham's, and Taylor's.
- **Opening Hours**: Varies by cellar, typically 10:00 AM – 6:00 PM.
- **Location**: Various locations in Vila Nova de Gaia, near the riverfront.
- **Fees**: €12–€30 (depending on the cellar and tasting options).

9. Serralves Foundation and Contemporary Art Museum

- **Highlights**:
  - A stunning contemporary art museum surrounded by beautifully landscaped gardens.
  - Hosts exhibitions, cultural events, and workshops.
- **Opening Hours**:
  - Tuesday to Sunday: 10:00 AM – 6:00 PM.
  - Closed on Mondays.
- **Location**: Rua Dom João de Castro 210, 4150-417 Porto, Portugal.
- **Fees**: €20 (includes museum and gardens).

---

10. Igreja de São Francisco (Church of Saint Francis)

- **Highlights**:
  - A Gothic church with an ornate baroque interior covered in gold leaf.
  - Houses a small museum and a crypt.
- **Opening Hours**:
  - Monday to Sunday: 9:00 AM – 7:00 PM.
- **Location**: Rua do Infante D. Henrique, 4050-297 Porto, Portugal.
- **Fees**: €7 per person.

Tips for Visiting Porto Attractions

1. **Timing**: Visit popular attractions like Livraria Lello and the Ribeira early in the day to avoid crowds.
2. **Tickets**: Book tickets online where possible to skip queues, especially during peak tourist seasons.
3. **Comfort**: Porto's hilly streets require comfortable walking shoes.
4. **Transportation**: Use public transportation or taxis to navigate between attractions efficiently.

Porto offers a perfect blend of historic charm and modern vibrancy, making it a must-visit destination for travelers seeking a unique and memorable experience.

Locate Attractions in Porto

Exploring Ribeira and the Douro River

Ribeira, Porto's historic riverside district, is the heart and soul of the city. With its colorful buildings, narrow cobblestone streets, and lively atmosphere, this UNESCO World Heritage Site offers a perfect starting point for your Porto adventure. Alongside the stunning Douro River, Ribeira is a vibrant blend of history, culture, and relaxation. Here's how to make the most of your time exploring Ribeira and the Douro River.

Discovering Ribeira's Charm

1. Wander the Riverside Promenade

- Take a leisurely stroll along Cais da Ribeira, Porto's picturesque waterfront. Enjoy the stunning views of the Dom Luís I Bridge and Vila Nova de Gaia on the opposite riverbank.
- Stop at one of the many outdoor cafés and restaurants for a traditional meal like *bacalhau à Brás* (salt cod) or *francesinha* (a hearty sandwich).

2. Admire the Architecture

- Ribeira is known for its colorful facades, many of which are adorned with traditional azulejo tiles. The narrow streets and alleys create a maze worth exploring.
- Look out for historic landmarks like Casa do Infante, where Prince Henry the Navigator was born.

3. Shop for Local Souvenirs

- Browse small shops and markets for handcrafted goods, including cork products, ceramics, and unique souvenirs.

Activities Along the Douro River

1. Take a Douro River Cruise

- A river cruise is a must-do activity for a unique perspective of Porto and its surroundings. Popular options include:
    - **Six Bridges Cruise**: A 50-minute boat ride showcasing Porto's iconic bridges.

- **Day Trips to the Douro Valley**: Full-day tours featuring wine tastings and visits to vineyards.
- **Cost**: €15–€25 for a short cruise; €80–€150 for full-day trips.
- **Tips**: Book tickets in advance during peak seasons.

2. Cross the Dom Luís I Bridge

- Walk or take the metro across this iconic double-deck bridge. The upper deck offers breathtaking views of Porto and the Douro River, especially at sunset.

3. Visit Vila Nova de Gaia

- Cross the river to Vila Nova de Gaia, home to Porto's famous wine cellars. Explore cellars like Taylor's, Sandeman, and Graham's, where you can enjoy port wine tastings and learn about its production.
- **Fees**: €12–€30 per tasting session, depending on the cellar.

Cultural Highlights in Ribeira

1. Ribeira Square (Praça da Ribeira)

- A vibrant gathering spot surrounded by restaurants and bars. The square is a perfect place to relax and soak in the lively atmosphere.

2. Igreja de São Nicolau

- A charming baroque church in the Ribeira area, offering a glimpse into Porto's religious heritage.

3. The Ribeira Wharf

- This historic port area was once the center of Porto's trade and maritime activities. Now it's a bustling area filled with life and energy.

Dining Along the Douro

1. Local Restaurants

- Try traditional dishes at riverside restaurants like Ribeira Square's *Postigo do Carvão* or *Chez Lapin*.
- Pair your meal with a glass of port or a refreshing vinho verde.

2. Riverside Bars

- Enjoy a relaxed evening at a wine bar overlooking the river. Popular spots include *Wine Quay Bar* and *Arco das Verdades*.

Tips for Exploring Ribeira and the Douro River

1. **Best Time to Visit**: Early morning or late afternoon offers fewer crowds and better lighting for photos.
2. **Comfortable Shoes**: Ribeira's cobblestone streets and hilly terrain require sturdy, comfortable footwear.
3. **Stay Hydrated**: Especially in summer, carry water as you explore the area.
4. **Sunset Views**: Head to the upper deck of Dom Luís I Bridge or Miradouro da Serra do Pilar in Vila Nova de Gaia for unforgettable sunsets over Ribeira and the Douro.

Exploring Ribeira and the Douro River is a magical experience that captures the essence of Porto. Whether you're savoring local cuisine, cruising the river, or wandering its historic streets, Ribeira is a place you'll never forget.

Gastronomic Delights in Porto

Porto is a culinary haven, where traditional Portuguese flavors meet contemporary gastronomic innovation. From hearty classics like *francesinha* to fresh seafood and indulgent pastries, the city offers a wide array of culinary experiences to satisfy every palate. Here's a guide to Porto's top gastronomic delights and where to find them.

Porto's Signature Dishes

1. Francesinha

- A decadent sandwich layered with ham, sausage, steak, and cheese, smothered in a rich beer-based sauce.
- **Where to Try**:
    - **Café Santiago**: Known as the gold standard for francesinha.
    - **Bufete Fase**: A no-frills spot specializing in this hearty dish.

2. Bacalhau (Codfish)

- Portugal's beloved salted cod, prepared in countless ways. Popular variations include *bacalhau à Brás* and *bacalhau com natas*.
- **Where to Try**:
    - **Adega São Nicolau**: Famous for its perfectly prepared bacalhau dishes.
    - **O Gaveto**: Exceptional seafood-focused restaurant in nearby Matosinhos.

3. Tripas à Moda do Porto

- A traditional tripe stew made with beans, sausage, and spices—a dish that showcases Porto's culinary heritage.
- **Where to Try**:
    - **O Buraco**: A family-run spot for authentic Portuguese comfort food.
    - **Abadia do Porto**: Offers a refined take on classic dishes, including tripas.

4. Caldo Verde

- A comforting soup made with kale, potatoes, and chorizo, often served as a starter.
- **Where to Try**:
    - **Taberna Santo António**: A cozy spot serving some of the best caldo verde in Porto.

5. Port Wine Desserts

- Porto's sweet treats often incorporate port wine, such as port-infused cheesecake or chocolate truffles.
- **Where to Try**:
    - **Tavi Confeitaria da Foz**: Offers elegant desserts with a view of the ocean.

Top Restaurants in Porto

1. The Yeatman Restaurant

- **Cuisine**: Fine dining with a focus on contemporary Portuguese flavors.
- **Highlights**: Michelin-starred dining with stunning views of the Douro River.
- **Location**: Rua do Choupelo, Vila Nova de Gaia.
- **Cost**: Tasting menus start at €140 per person.

2. O Paparico

- **Cuisine**: Upscale Portuguese cuisine served in a cozy, rustic setting.
- **Highlights**: Creative interpretations of traditional dishes.
- **Location**: Rua de Costa Cabral 2343, 4200-232 Porto.
- **Cost**: €50–€100 per person.

3. Cantina 32

- **Cuisine**: Modern Portuguese tapas with international influences.
- **Highlights**: Trendy ambiance and must-try dishes like oxtail and octopus.
- **Location**: Rua das Flores 32, 4050-262 Porto.
- **Cost**: €25–€40 per person.

4. Mito

- **Cuisine**: Innovative, seasonal dishes with global inspiration.
- **Highlights**: Casual fine dining with a constantly changing menu.
- **Location**: Rua de José Falcão 183, 4050-317 Porto.
- **Cost**: €20–€40 per person.

5. Pedro Lemos

- **Cuisine**: Haute cuisine using locally sourced ingredients.
- **Highlights**: Michelin-starred restaurant in a charming townhouse.
- **Location**: Rua do Padre Luís Cabral 974, 4150-459 Porto.
- **Cost**: Tasting menus from €125 per person.

Sweet Treats and Pastry Shops

1. Pastéis de Nata (Custard Tarts)

- A must-try Portuguese pastry with a creamy custard filling in a flaky crust.
- **Where to Try**:
  - **Fábrica da Nata**: Renowned for its freshly baked pastéis de nata.
  - **Manteigaria**: Another popular spot for these delicious tarts.

2. Bolinhos de Bacalhau (Codfish Cakes)

- Perfect for a snack on the go or as an appetizer.
- **Where to Try**:
  - **Casa Portuguesa do Pastel de Bacalhau**: Famous for its codfish cakes paired with port wine.

3. Rabanadas (Portuguese French Toast)

- A festive dessert often enjoyed during Christmas, but available year-round in Porto.
- **Where to Try**:
  - **Confeitaria do Bolhão**: A historic bakery serving traditional Portuguese sweets.

Food Markets and Culinary Experiences
1. Mercado do Bolhão

- **Highlights**: A historic market where you can buy fresh produce, seafood, and local delicacies.
- **Location**: Rua Formosa, 4000-214 Porto.
- **Opening Hours**: Monday to Saturday, 8:00 AM – 8:00 PM.
- **Fees**: Free entry.

2. Wine and Food Tours

- Join a guided tour to sample Porto's culinary offerings, from street food to port wine pairings.
- Popular options:
  - **Taste Porto Food Tours**
  - **Douro Valley Wine Tours**

Dining Tips for Porto

1. **Reservation**: Book in advance for popular restaurants, especially Michelin-starred ones.
2. **Local Specialties**: Don't miss dishes like *francesinha* or *bacalhau*.
3. **Port Wine Pairings**: Most meals can be enhanced with a glass of Porto's famous port wine.

Porto's culinary scene is a celebration of Portuguese traditions and modern creativity, offering travelers a rich and flavorful journey. Bon appétit!

Day Trips from Porto

Porto's central location makes it an excellent base for exploring northern Portugal's breathtaking landscapes, historic towns, and cultural landmarks. Whether you're into wine tasting, medieval castles, or coastal scenery, these day trips offer something for everyone.

1. Douro Valley

- **Highlights**:
    - A UNESCO World Heritage Site, known for its terraced vineyards and port wine production.
    - Enjoy wine tastings at prestigious estates, take a scenic boat cruise along the Douro River, or drive through picturesque villages.
- **Distance**: ~100 km (1.5–2 hours by car).
- **How to Get There**: Guided tours, car, or train to Peso da Régua.
- **Tip**: Book a river cruise or private wine tour for the full experience.

---

2. Braga

- **Highlights**:
    - Known as the "Rome of Portugal," Braga is rich in religious history with its stunning churches and sanctuaries.
    - Visit the iconic Bom Jesus do Monte, a baroque masterpiece with an impressive staircase.
    - Explore Braga Cathedral and enjoy the vibrant city center.

- **Distance**: ~55 km (1 hour by car or train).
- **How to Get There**: Direct train from Porto's São Bento station.
- **Fees**: Free to explore; Bom Jesus funicular costs around €1.50.

---

3. Guimarães

- **Highlights**:
    - The birthplace of Portugal, home to a well-preserved medieval center (UNESCO-listed).
    - Visit Guimarães Castle, the Palace of the Dukes of Braganza, and Largo da Oliveira.
- **Distance**: ~50 km (1 hour by car or train).
- **How to Get There**: Direct train from Porto's São Bento station.
- **Fees**: Entry to Guimarães Castle (€2) and Palace of the Dukes (€5).

---

4. Aveiro and Costa Nova

- **Highlights**:
    - Aveiro is often called the "Venice of Portugal" for its picturesque canals and colorful *moliceiro* boats.
    - Nearby Costa Nova is famous for its striped beach houses and stunning coastline.
- **Distance**: ~75 km (1 hour by car or train).
- **How to Get There**: Direct train from Porto's Campanhã station.
- **Fees**: Boat rides cost around €10–€15.

---

5. Viana do Castelo

- **Highlights**:
    - A charming coastal town known for its scenic beauty and cultural heritage.
    - Visit the Basilica of Santa Luzia for panoramic views, and explore the historic center.
- **Distance**: ~75 km (1 hour by car).
- **How to Get There**: Car or train (with a transfer in Nine).
- **Tip**: Combine your visit with a trip to nearby beaches.

6. Peneda-Gerês National Park

- **Highlights**:
  - Portugal's only national park, offering lush forests, cascading waterfalls, and scenic hiking trails.
  - Explore Soajo's ancient granaries and visit natural pools like Cascata do Arado.
- **Distance**: ~100 km (1.5 hours by car).
- **How to Get There**: Best reached by car or with a guided tour.
- **Tip**: Wear comfortable hiking shoes and bring swimwear for the natural pools.

---

7. Santiago de Compostela (Spain)

- **Highlights**:
  - A renowned pilgrimage site, featuring the stunning Santiago de Compostela Cathedral.
  - Wander the old town, a UNESCO World Heritage Site.
- **Distance**: ~230 km (2.5 hours by car).
- **How to Get There**: Guided tours or drive.
- **Fees**: Free to enter the cathedral; tours cost extra.

---

8. Espinho

- **Highlights**:
  - A beachside town known for its golden sands and seafood restaurants.
  - Visit the weekly open-air market, one of the largest in Portugal.
- **Distance**: ~20 km (30 minutes by car or train).
- **How to Get There**: Direct train from Porto's São Bento station.
- **Tip**: Best for a relaxed seaside escape.

---

9. Coimbra

- **Highlights**:
  - One of Portugal's oldest cities, famous for its historic university and stunning Joanina Library.
  - Visit the Old Cathedral and climb the tower for city views.

- **Distance**: ~120 km (1.5 hours by car or train).
- **How to Get There**: Direct train from Porto's Campanhã station.
- **Fees**: University tours cost around €12.

---

10. Matosinhos

- **Highlights**:
    - A seafood lover's paradise, with some of the freshest catches in Portugal.
    - Enjoy the expansive beach and coastal promenade.
- **Distance**: ~10 km (20 minutes by metro).
- **How to Get There**: Metro Line A from Porto.
- **Fees**: Free to explore; meals vary by restaurant.

Tips for Day Trips from Porto

1. **Transportation**: Consider trains for convenience or guided tours for a hassle-free experience.
2. **Timing**: Start early to make the most of your day, especially for destinations like the Douro Valley or Santiago de Compostela.
3. **Packing**: Bring comfortable walking shoes, a water bottle, and weather-appropriate clothing.
4. **Local Guides**: Opt for guided tours for deeper insights into the history and culture of these locations.

From coastal retreats to historic landmarks, Porto's surroundings promise unforgettable adventures for every traveler.

Locate Restaurants in Porto

Chapter 7: Lisbon: The City of Light

Must-See Landmarks in Lisbon

Lisbon, the sunlit capital of Portugal, is a city steeped in history, culture, and breathtaking architecture. From iconic monuments to picturesque neighborhoods, the city offers a wealth of landmarks that showcase its rich heritage and charm. Here's a guide to the must-see landmarks in Lisbon:

1. Belém Tower (Torre de Belém)

- **Highlights**:
    - A UNESCO World Heritage Site, this 16th-century fortress symbolizes Portugal's Age of Discovery.
    - Features intricate Manueline architecture and stunning views of the Tagus River.
- **Location**: Avenida Brasília, Belém.
- **Opening Hours**:
    - October–April: 10:00 AM – 5:30 PM (last entry 5:00 PM).
    - May–September: 10:00 AM – 6:30 PM (last entry 6:00 PM).
- **Fees**: €6 (discounts for students and seniors).

---

2. Jerónimos Monastery (Mosteiro dos Jerónimos)

- **Highlights**:
    - A masterpiece of Manueline architecture, built to honor Vasco da Gama's voyage to India.
    - Houses the tombs of Vasco da Gama and Luís de Camões, Portugal's literary icon.
- **Location**: Praça do Império, Belém.
- **Opening Hours**:
    - October–April: 10:00 AM – 5:30 PM (last entry 5:00 PM).
    - May–September: 10:00 AM – 6:30 PM (last entry 6:00 PM).
- **Fees**: €10 (combo tickets with other Belém sites available).

3. São Jorge Castle (Castelo de São Jorge)

- **Highlights**:
    - Perched on a hilltop, this medieval castle offers panoramic views of Lisbon's cityscape.
    - Explore ancient walls, archaeological sites, and watch peacocks roam the grounds.
- **Location**: Rua de Santa Cruz do Castelo.
- **Opening Hours**: 9:00 AM – 9:00 PM.
- **Fees**: €10 (discounts for students and seniors).

---

4. Alfama District

- **Highlights**:
    - Lisbon's oldest neighborhood, known for its narrow, winding streets, colorful houses, and traditional *fado* music.
    - Key landmarks include the Lisbon Cathedral (*Sé de Lisboa*) and Miradouro da Senhora do Monte, a popular viewpoint.
- **Location**: Alfama is a short walk from São Jorge Castle.
- **Fees**: Free to explore; guided tours available for deeper insights.

---

5. Praça do Comércio (Commerce Square)

- **Highlights**:
    - A grand waterfront square framed by elegant arcades and the iconic Arco da Rua Augusta.
    - Once the site of the royal palace, it's now a bustling hub of restaurants and cafes.
- **Location**: Baixa district.
- **Fees**: Free to visit; access to the Arco da Rua Augusta viewpoint costs €3.

---

6. Santa Justa Lift (Elevador de Santa Justa)

- **Highlights**:
    - A neo-Gothic elevator offering a unique way to connect Baixa to the Bairro Alto district.
    - Provides spectacular views of the city from its top platform.
- **Location**: Rua do Ouro.
- **Opening Hours**: 7:00 AM – 10:00 PM.
- **Fees**: €5.30 (includes round trip and access to the viewing platform).

---

7. Bairro Alto and Chiado

- **Highlights**:
    - Bairro Alto is famous for its vibrant nightlife and traditional *tascas* (taverns).
    - Chiado offers an artistic flair with theaters, boutiques, and historic cafes like Café A Brasileira.
- **Location**: Central Lisbon, easily accessible by tram or on foot.
- **Fees**: Free to explore; bar and shop prices vary.

---

8. Padrão dos Descobrimentos (Monument to the Discoveries)

- **Highlights**:
    - A striking riverside monument commemorating Portugal's explorers, shaped like a ship's prow.
    - Climb to the top for sweeping views of Belém and the Tagus River.
- **Location**: Avenida Brasília, Belém.
- **Opening Hours**:
    - October–April: 10:00 AM – 5:30 PM.
    - May–September: 10:00 AM – 6:30 PM.
- **Fees**: €6 (discounts available).

9. National Tile Museum (Museu Nacional do Azulejo)

- **Highlights**:
  - Dedicated to Portugal's famous *azulejos* (ceramic tiles), showcasing their evolution over five centuries.
  - Features a stunning tiled panorama of Lisbon before the 1755 earthquake.
- **Location**: Rua da Madre de Deus 4.
- **Opening Hours**: 10:00 AM – 6:00 PM (closed Mondays).
- **Fees**: €5.

---

10. Parque das Nações

- **Highlights**:
  - A modern district transformed for Expo '98, featuring the Oceanário de Lisboa, one of the world's largest aquariums.
  - Stroll along the waterfront promenade or ride the cable car for views of the Vasco da Gama Bridge.
- **Location**: Northeast Lisbon.
- **Fees**: Free to explore; Oceanarium entry costs €19.

Tips for Visiting Lisbon's Landmarks

1. **Plan Ahead**: Many landmarks have long lines—buy tickets online to save time.
2. **Wear Comfortable Shoes**: Lisbon's hilly terrain and cobblestone streets require good footwear.
3. **Take Public Transport**: Use trams, buses, or metro to navigate the city easily.
4. **Visit Early or Late**: Avoid crowds by visiting popular sites during off-peak hours.

Lisbon's landmarks tell the story of its maritime heritage, cultural vibrancy, and architectural splendor. Make time to explore these treasures and discover the soul of the city.

Attractions in Lisbon

Hidden Gems and Local Neighborhoods in Lisbon

While Lisbon's famous landmarks attract the crowds, the city is brimming with hidden gems and charming neighborhoods waiting to be explored. These off-the-beaten-path spots and local areas reveal a more intimate, authentic side of Portugal's capital.

Hidden Gems

1. LX Factory

- **Highlights**:
  - A former industrial complex transformed into a creative hub filled with trendy cafes, unique boutiques, art galleries, and street art.
  - Don't miss Ler Devagar, a stunning bookstore with a suspended bicycle sculpture.
- **Location**: Alcântara neighborhood.
- **Tip**: Visit on Sundays for the outdoor market featuring local artisans and food vendors.

2. Estrela Basilica and Garden

- **Highlights**:
  - A less-touristy baroque church with a striking dome offering panoramic views of the city.
  - Adjacent to it is Jardim da Estrela, a peaceful garden perfect for a leisurely stroll.
- **Location**: Estrela neighborhood.
- **Tip**: Visit in the late afternoon for beautiful lighting inside the basilica.

3. Museu da Água (Water Museum)

- **Highlights**:
  - A fascinating museum dedicated to Lisbon's water supply system, including the Águas Livres Aqueduct, an architectural marvel from the 18th century.
  - Walk across the aqueduct for a unique experience and stunning views.
- **Location**: Campolide neighborhood.
- **Tip**: Combine your visit with a walk to nearby Amoreiras for panoramic city views from the Amoreiras 360 viewpoint.

4. Feira da Ladra (Thieves' Market)

- **Highlights**:
    - Lisbon's oldest flea market, held twice a week (Tuesdays and Saturdays).
    - Browse vintage treasures, antiques, and quirky items while soaking in the lively atmosphere.
- **Location**: Campo de Santa Clara, near the National Pantheon.
- **Tip**: Arrive early for the best finds and bring cash for bargaining.

5. Tapada das Necessidades

- **Highlights**:
    - A serene, lesser-known park with shaded trails, exotic plants, and ruins of old greenhouses.
    - Ideal for picnics and quiet escapes from the city buzz.
- **Location**: Alcântara neighborhood.
- **Tip**: Bring snacks or drinks as there aren't many nearby vendors.

Local Neighborhoods to Explore

1. Graça

- **Vibe**: Authentic, laid-back, and scenic.
- **Highlights**:
    - Two of Lisbon's best viewpoints (*miradouros*): Miradouro da Senhora do Monte and Miradouro da Graça.
    - Charming streets, small shops, and local restaurants.
- **Tip**: Visit at sunset for breathtaking views of the city and the Tagus River.

2. Campo de Ourique

- **Vibe**: Residential, trendy, and family-friendly.
- **Highlights**:
    - Campo de Ourique Market, where you can sample delicious Portuguese dishes and desserts.
    - A relaxed atmosphere with fewer tourists and excellent local cafes.
- **Tip**: Try the pastel de nata from Aloma, one of Lisbon's best pastry shops.

3. Mouraria

- **Vibe**: Multicultural, historic, and vibrant.
- **Highlights**:
    - The birthplace of *fado* music, with narrow streets adorned with murals and cultural landmarks.
    - A variety of international eateries, reflecting Lisbon's diverse community.
- **Tip**: Explore Rua do Capelão for street art and stop by tiny bars with live *fado* performances.

4. Alcântara

- **Vibe**: Industrial-chic and artistic.
- **Highlights**:
    - Home to LX Factory and vibrant nightlife options.
    - Explore the riverside promenade and check out Pilar 7 Bridge Experience, where you can walk inside the 25 de Abril Bridge.
- **Tip**: Stop at Village Underground Lisbon for a drink in a quirky setting made of repurposed buses and containers.

5. Madragoa

- **Vibe**: Quaint, historic, and local-focused.
- **Highlights**:
    - A peaceful neighborhood with colorful houses, azulejo-covered buildings, and traditional taverns.
    - Nearby attractions include the National Museum of Ancient Art.
- **Tip**: Dine at a small *tasca* (traditional eatery) for an authentic Portuguese meal.

6. Ajuda

- **Vibe**: Historic and regal.
- **Highlights**:
    - The Ajuda National Palace, a stunning royal residence filled with opulent decor.
    - Jardim Botânico da Ajuda, Lisbon's oldest botanical garden.
- **Tip**: Combine your visit with a stop at the nearby Belém attractions.

Tips for Discovering Lisbon's Hidden Gems and Local Neighborhoods

1. **Use Public Transport**: Many of these areas are accessible by tram, bus, or metro.
2. **Take Your Time**: Stroll leisurely and explore side streets to uncover surprises.
3. **Engage with Locals**: Small cafes and family-run shops are great places to chat with locals for insider tips.
4. **Go Beyond the Center**: Neighborhoods like Ajuda and Campo de Ourique offer a different perspective of Lisbon life.

Exploring these lesser-known spots and neighborhoods will deepen your appreciation of Lisbon's diverse culture and hidden treasures, making your trip even more memorable.

Where to Eat in Lisbon

Lisbon is a food lover's paradise, offering everything from traditional Portuguese dishes to contemporary cuisine. Whether you're craving fresh seafood, hearty comfort food, or sweet treats, the city's diverse culinary scene caters to all tastes. Here's a guide to the best places to eat in Lisbon, spanning local favorites, trendy hotspots, and hidden gems.

Traditional Portuguese Restaurants

1. Ramiro

- **What to Eat**: Famous for its seafood, especially the garlic butter prawns, clams, and scarlet shrimp.
- **Highlights**: An iconic Lisbon institution for seafood lovers.
- **Location**: Av. Almirante Reis 1, Intendente.
- **Price Range**: €30–€50 per person.
- **Tip**: Arrive early or be prepared for a wait—it's worth it.

2. Taberna da Rua das Flores

- **What to Eat**: Seasonal tapas-style dishes inspired by Portuguese cuisine, like *bacalhau à brás* and pork cheeks.
- **Highlights**: A cozy, intimate eatery with a menu that changes daily.
- **Location**: Rua das Flores 103, Chiado.
- **Price Range**: €20–€40 per person.
- **Tip**: No reservations—go early to secure a table.

3. A Cevicheria

- **What to Eat**: Innovative Peruvian-Portuguese fusion dishes, especially the signature ceviche and pisco sour.
- **Highlights**: A trendy spot with a giant octopus sculpture hanging from the ceiling.
- **Location**: Rua Dom Pedro V 129, Príncipe Real.
- **Price Range**: €30–€50 per person.
- **Tip**: Ideal for adventurous foodies looking for a unique dining experience.

Best for Petiscos (Portuguese Tapas)

4. BA Wine Bar do Bairro Alto

- **What to Eat**: Try a curated selection of Portuguese wines paired with cheeses, cured meats, and sardines.
- **Highlights**: Small and charming, perfect for wine enthusiasts.
- **Location**: Rua da Rosa 107, Bairro Alto.
- **Price Range**: €20–€40 per person.
- **Tip**: Reservations are essential due to its small size.

5. O Velho Eurico

- **What to Eat**: Classic dishes like *peixinhos da horta* (fried green beans) and hearty soups.
- **Highlights**: A laid-back eatery known for its authentic flavors and casual vibe.
- **Location**: Largo São Cristóvão 3, Mouraria.
- **Price Range**: €15–€30 per person.
- **Tip**: Order several small plates to share and enjoy a variety of flavors.

Top Contemporary and Fine Dining Spots

6. Belcanto

- **What to Eat**: José Avillez's Michelin-starred creations, such as codfish à la Brás and the Mandarin dessert.
- **Highlights**: One of Lisbon's most prestigious fine dining experiences.
- **Location**: Largo de São Carlos 10, Chiado.
- **Price Range**: €150+ per person.

- **Tip**: Book well in advance for this exclusive dining experience.

7. Prado

- **What to Eat**: Farm-to-table dishes emphasizing fresh, seasonal, and sustainable ingredients.
- **Highlights**: A minimalist yet elegant restaurant with an ever-changing menu.
- **Location**: Travessa das Pedras Negras 2, Alfama.
- **Price Range**: €40–€60 per person.
- **Tip**: The house-made sourdough bread is a must-try.

Budget-Friendly Eateries

8. Time Out Market

- **What to Eat**: A variety of dishes from different vendors, including *prego* sandwiches, seafood, and pastries.
- **Highlights**: A lively food hall showcasing Lisbon's best culinary talent.
- **Location**: Av. 24 de Julho, Cais do Sodré.
- **Price Range**: €10–€30 per person.
- **Tip**: Great for groups with varied tastes.

9. Casa da Índia

- **What to Eat**: Roast chicken, fries, and rice—simple yet delicious Portuguese comfort food.
- **Highlights**: A bustling local spot with no-frills dining.
- **Location**: Rua do Loreto 49, Chiado.
- **Price Range**: €10–€20 per person.
- **Tip**: Perfect for a quick, hearty meal on a budget.

Sweet Treats and Desserts

10. Pastéis de Belém

- **What to Eat**: The original *pastéis de nata* (custard tarts).
- **Highlights**: Made fresh daily using a secret recipe from the 1830s.
- **Location**: Rua de Belém 84–92, Belém.
- **Price Range**: €1.50 per tart.
- **Tip**: Eat them warm with a sprinkle of cinnamon and powdered sugar.

11. Manteigaria

- **What to Eat**: *Pastéis de nata* that rival those of Belém.
- **Highlights**: Watch the tarts being made fresh behind the counter.
- **Location**: Rua do Loreto 2, Chiado.
- **Price Range**: €1.50 per tart.
- **Tip**: Perfect for a quick sweet treat while exploring the city.

Tips for Dining in Lisbon

1. **Reservations**: Popular spots often require reservations, especially for dinner.
2. **Timing**: Many restaurants open for lunch from 12:30–3:00 PM and dinner from 7:30 PM onward.
3. **Shared Dishes**: Don't hesitate to order multiple dishes for the table—Portuguese dining is often a communal experience.
4. **Cover Charges**: Bread, olives, and other starters may appear unrequested but are not free. Accept or decline based on your preference.

Lisbon's culinary landscape offers something for every palate and budget. From traditional *tascas* to Michelin-starred dining, the city is a feast for the senses, ensuring an unforgettable gastronomic journey.

Top Day Trips from Lisbon

Lisbon's central location makes it the perfect base for exploring some of Portugal's most stunning destinations. Whether you're interested in picturesque towns, historical landmarks, or coastal retreats, these day trips offer a glimpse into the rich culture and natural beauty just beyond the city.

1. Sintra

- **Highlights**:
    - **Pena Palace**: A fairytale-like palace with vibrant colors and panoramic views.
    - **Quinta da Regaleira**: A mystical estate with gardens, grottoes, and the famous Initiation Well.
    - **Moorish Castle**: Ancient ruins perched on a hilltop offering incredible vistas.
- **Travel Time**: 40 minutes by train from Lisbon (Rossio Station).
- **Tips**: Wear comfortable shoes, as Sintra involves a lot of walking. Start early to visit multiple attractions.

---

2. Cascais

- **Highlights**:
    - **Praia da Rainha**: A small, beautiful beach perfect for relaxation.
    - **Boca do Inferno**: A dramatic cliff formation with waves crashing into caves.
    - **Cascais Marina**: A picturesque spot with seafood restaurants and charming streets.
- **Travel Time**: 40 minutes by train from Lisbon (Cais do Sodré Station).
- **Tips**: Combine Cascais with a visit to Estoril, a nearby coastal town known for its casino and sandy beaches.

---

3. Belém

- **Highlights**:
    - **Jerónimos Monastery**: A UNESCO World Heritage site showcasing stunning Manueline architecture.
    - **Belém Tower**: A fortified tower on the banks of the Tagus River.
    - **Pastéis de Belém**: Enjoy the famous custard tarts at their original home.
- **Travel Time**: 15 minutes by tram or bus from central Lisbon.
- **Tips**: Visit early in the day to avoid crowds at the monastery and tower.

---

4. Évora

- **Highlights**:
    - **Roman Temple**: A well-preserved Roman-era structure in the heart of the city.
    - **Chapel of Bones**: A hauntingly beautiful chapel lined with human bones.
    - **Évora Cathedral**: A blend of Romanesque and Gothic architecture.
- **Travel Time**: 1.5 hours by car or train from Lisbon.
- **Tips**: Évora is part of the Alentejo region, so consider sampling local wines and dishes.

---

5. Óbidos

- **Highlights**:
    - **Medieval Castle**: Explore the cobblestone streets and walk along the castle walls.
    - **Ginja Liqueur**: Sip this traditional cherry liqueur served in edible chocolate cups.
    - **Bookshops**: Unique stores set in historic locations, such as a church-turned-library.
- **Travel Time**: 1 hour by car or bus from Lisbon.
- **Tips**: Time your visit during the annual Óbidos Chocolate Festival (March–April) or the Christmas Village event.

---

6. Fátima

- **Highlights**:
  - **Sanctuary of Fátima**: A major pilgrimage site known for the apparitions of the Virgin Mary.
  - **Basilica of the Holy Trinity**: A modern architectural marvel.
  - **Chapel of the Apparitions**: The spiritual heart of the sanctuary.
- **Travel Time**: 1.5 hours by car or bus from Lisbon.
- **Tips**: Visit on the 13th of the month (May–October) for special religious ceremonies.

---

7. Setúbal and Arrábida Natural Park

- **Highlights**:
  - **Arrábida Beaches**: Pristine beaches like Portinho da Arrábida, surrounded by turquoise waters and green hills.
  - **Setúbal Market**: A lively market offering fresh seafood and local delicacies.
  - **Dolphin Watching**: Take a boat tour to spot dolphins in the Sado Estuary.
- **Travel Time**: 1 hour by car or bus from Lisbon.
- **Tips**: Bring a swimsuit and pack a picnic for the beaches.

---

8. Nazaré

- **Highlights**:
  - **Big Waves**: Watch surfers tackle some of the world's biggest waves at Praia do Norte.
  - **Nossa Senhora da Nazaré Sanctuary**: A clifftop church with incredible ocean views.
  - **Local Cuisine**: Sample fresh seafood, including grilled sardines and octopus stew.
- **Travel Time**: 1.5 hours by car or bus from Lisbon.
- **Tips**: Best visited in winter when the waves are at their peak for surf enthusiasts.

9. Tomar

- **Highlights**:
  - **Convent of Christ**: A UNESCO World Heritage site and former Templar stronghold.
  - **Tomar Old Town**: Wander through charming streets filled with history.
  - **Pegões Aqueduct**: An impressive 17th-century aqueduct on the outskirts of town.
- **Travel Time**: 2 hours by car or train from Lisbon.
- **Tips**: Combine Tomar with a visit to nearby Almourol Castle for a day immersed in history.

---

10. Peniche and Berlengas Islands

- **Highlights**:
  - **Surfing**: Peniche is one of Portugal's top surfing destinations.
  - **Berlengas Islands**: A stunning archipelago ideal for hiking, snorkeling, and exploring the Fort of São João Baptista.
- **Travel Time**: 1.5 hours by car to Peniche, followed by a 30-minute boat ride to the islands.
- **Tips**: Book your boat trip to Berlengas in advance, especially during the summer.

Tips for Day Trips from Lisbon

1. **Plan Ahead**: Check transportation schedules and ticket availability for popular destinations.
2. **Start Early**: Maximize your time by leaving Lisbon in the morning.
3. **Dress Comfortably**: Many destinations involve walking or outdoor activities, so wear appropriate shoes and clothing.
4. **Pack Essentials**: Bring water, snacks, sunscreen, and a camera to capture the sights.

With so many incredible destinations within easy reach, Lisbon's day trips offer something for everyone, from history buffs to nature lovers. These adventures will add depth and diversity to your Portuguese journey.

Chapter 8: Outdoor and Adventure Activities

Beaches Near Porto and Lisbon

Portugal is renowned for its stunning coastline, and both Porto and Lisbon offer easy access to some of the country's most beautiful beaches. Whether you're looking for sandy stretches to relax on, dramatic cliffs, or spots for water sports, there's a beach for everyone.

Beaches Near Porto

1. Matosinhos Beach

- **Highlights**: A wide, sandy beach ideal for surfing and sunbathing. Popular among locals for its seafood restaurants.
- **Location**: 20 minutes by metro from Porto city center.
- **Best For**: Surfing, beginner-friendly lessons, casual dining.
- **Facilities**: Surf schools, showers, and lifeguards during summer.

2. Praia de Miramar

- **Highlights**: Known for the Capela do Senhor da Pedra, a picturesque chapel perched on a rock by the sea.
- **Location**: 15 km south of Porto, accessible by train.
- **Best For**: Scenic beauty, peaceful atmosphere.
- **Facilities**: Limited, so pack essentials for a day trip.

3. Praia de Leça da Palmeira

- **Highlights**: A quieter alternative to Matosinhos with a dramatic rocky coastline and tidal pools.
- **Location**: 10 km from Porto, reachable by car or metro.
- **Best For**: Relaxation and photography.
- **Facilities**: Cafés and small restaurants nearby.

4. Praia da Aguda

- **Highlights**: A charming fishing village with a long stretch of golden sand and great seafood options.
- **Location**: 20 km south of Porto, accessible by train.
- **Best For**: Couples, peaceful escapes.
- **Facilities**: A few local restaurants and cafés.

5. Espinho Beach

- **Highlights**: A bustling beach town with a casino and a weekly outdoor market.
- **Location**: 25 km south of Porto, accessible by train.
- **Best For**: Families, surfing, and local shopping.
- **Facilities**: Restaurants, surf schools, and lifeguards.

Beaches Near Lisbon

1. Cascais Beaches (Praia da Conceição and Praia da Rainha)

- **Highlights**: Small, sandy beaches located in the heart of Cascais, perfect for swimming and relaxing.
- **Location**: 40 minutes by train from Lisbon (Cais do Sodré).
- **Best For**: Convenience, family outings.
- **Facilities**: Cafés, restaurants, and rental chairs available.

2. Praia do Guincho

- **Highlights**: A windswept beach famous for surfing, kitesurfing, and windsurfing, surrounded by the Serra de Sintra.
- **Location**: 10 km from Cascais, reachable by bus or car.
- **Best For**: Water sports, dramatic scenery.
- **Facilities**: Surf schools, parking, and a few nearby restaurants.

3. Costa da Caparica

- **Highlights**: A long stretch of sandy beaches divided into different zones, ranging from family-friendly spots to trendy beach bars.
- **Location**: 20 minutes by car or ferry from Lisbon.
- **Best For**: Variety, nightlife, surfing.

- **Facilities**: Beach bars, restaurants, and lifeguards in summer.

4. Praia da Adraga

- **Highlights**: A hidden gem with dramatic cliffs and a secluded feel. Voted one of Europe's best beaches.
- **Location**: Near Sintra, about 45 minutes by car from Lisbon.
- **Best For**: Photography, peaceful retreats.
- **Facilities**: A small café and parking.

5. Praia de Carcavelos

- **Highlights**: One of the closest beaches to Lisbon, popular for swimming, beach volleyball, and surfing.
- **Location**: 20 minutes by train from Lisbon (Cais do Sodré).
- **Best For**: Convenience, beginners learning to surf.
- **Facilities**: Surf schools, showers, and plenty of dining options.

6. Praia do Meco

- **Highlights**: A naturist-friendly beach with pristine sand dunes and a relaxed atmosphere.
- **Location**: 40 minutes by car from Lisbon, near Sesimbra.
- **Best For**: Seclusion, natural beauty.
- **Facilities**: Limited, so bring supplies.

7. Praia do Tamariz

- **Highlights**: Located near Estoril, this beach is ideal for families and has calm waters for swimming.
- **Location**: 30 minutes by train from Lisbon.
- **Best For**: Families, easy access.
- **Facilities**: Restaurants, cafés, and sun lounger rentals.

Tips for Visiting Beaches

1. **Transportation**: Many beaches near Porto and Lisbon are accessible by train or car. Plan your route in advance.
2. **Season**: The best time to visit is from late spring to early autumn when the weather is warm and facilities are open.
3. **Essentials**: Bring sunscreen, water, and beachwear. Some beaches have limited facilities.
4. **Tides and Conditions**: Check local surf reports or tide schedules, especially if you're visiting for water sports.

Whether you're seeking lively beach towns or tranquil hidden coves, the beaches near Porto and Lisbon cater to all preferences, making them an unmissable part of your Portugal adventure.

Hiking Trails and Nature Escapes

Portugal's diverse landscapes offer breathtaking opportunities for hiking and connecting with nature. From dramatic cliffs and lush forests to river valleys and rolling hills, both Porto and Lisbon serve as gateways to stunning outdoor adventures. Whether you're a seasoned hiker or prefer a leisurely stroll, these trails and nature escapes near Porto and Lisbon provide unforgettable experiences.

Hiking Trails Near Porto

1. Peneda-Gerês National Park

- **Highlights**: Portugal's only national park features cascading waterfalls, dense forests, and granite peaks.
- **Top Trails**:
  - **Trilho da Preguiça**: A short, scenic trail perfect for beginners.
  - **Cascata do Arado Trail**: Leads to one of the park's most beautiful waterfalls.
- **Travel Time**: 1.5–2 hours by car from Porto.
- **Tips**: Wear sturdy shoes and pack water. Keep an eye out for wild ponies and ancient Roman roads.

2. Douro Valley Vineyards and Villages

- **Highlights**: A UNESCO World Heritage site with terraced vineyards and river views.
- **Top Trails**:
  - **São Salvador do Mundo Trail**: A moderate hike with panoramic vistas of the Douro River.
  - **Pinhão River Walk**: A gentle trail winding through vineyards and quaint villages.
- **Travel Time**: 1.5 hours by car or train from Porto.
- **Tips**: Combine your hike with a wine-tasting tour at a local quinta (winery).

3. Serra da Freita

- **Highlights**: Known for its unique geological formations, waterfalls, and traditional villages.
- **Top Trails**:
  - **Passadiços do Paiva**: A wooden boardwalk trail along the Paiva River, offering easy access to nature.
  - **Frecha da Mizarela Waterfall Trail**: A short hike to one of Portugal's tallest waterfalls.
- **Travel Time**: 1.5 hours by car from Porto.
- **Tips**: Book tickets in advance for Passadiços do Paiva, as entry is limited.

4. Arouca Geopark

- **Highlights**: A UNESCO-recognized park with dramatic suspension bridges, including the famous 516 Arouca.
- **Top Trails**:
  - **516 Arouca Suspension Bridge Walk**: A thrilling crossing paired with breathtaking views of the Aguieiras Waterfall.
- **Travel Time**: 1.5 hours by car from Porto.
- **Tips**: Check weather conditions before visiting for optimal views.

Hiking Trails Near Lisbon

1. Sintra-Cascais Natural Park

- **Highlights**: A mix of coastal cliffs, lush forests, and fairytale-like palaces.
- **Top Trails**:
    - **Cabo da Roca to Praia da Ursa**: A rugged coastal hike to one of Portugal's most beautiful beaches.
    - **Trail to Monserrate Palace**: A gentle walk through verdant gardens and exotic plants.
- **Travel Time**: 30–45 minutes by car or train from Lisbon.
- **Tips**: Start early to avoid crowds, especially in the summer months.

2. Arrábida Natural Park

- **Highlights**: Stunning coastal landscapes, turquoise waters, and serene trails.
- **Top Trails**:
    - **Serra do Risco Clifftop Walk**: A moderate hike with sweeping ocean views.
    - **Praia dos Coelhos Trail**: Leads to a secluded beach surrounded by dramatic cliffs.
- **Travel Time**: 40 minutes by car from Lisbon.
- **Tips**: Bring a swimsuit to enjoy a post-hike dip in the sea.

3. Tapada Nacional de Mafra

- **Highlights**: A royal hunting reserve featuring wildlife such as deer and wild boar, along with shaded forest paths.
- **Top Trails**:
    - **Wildlife Observation Trail**: Perfect for families, with opportunities to spot native animals.
- **Travel Time**: 30 minutes by car from Lisbon.
- **Tips**: Visit the nearby Mafra Palace for a mix of history and nature.

4. Cabo Espichel

- **Highlights**: A remote cape with dramatic cliffs and stunning ocean views.
- **Top Trails**:
    - **Dinosaur Footprint Trail**: A fascinating walk that passes ancient fossilized tracks.

- **Travel Time**: 1 hour by car from Lisbon.
- **Tips**: The area can get windy, so bring a light jacket.

5. Cascais to Guincho Trail

- **Highlights**: A scenic coastal path perfect for an easy, leisurely hike.
- **Top Trails**:
  - **Ciclovia Cascais-Guincho**: A paved trail offering ocean views and accessibility for bikes as well.
- **Travel Time**: 40 minutes by train from Lisbon to Cascais.
- **Tips**: Stop at Guincho Beach for a refreshing break or a meal at a beachside café.

Tips for Hiking in Portugal

1. **Gear Up**: Wear comfortable hiking shoes, and bring sunscreen, water, and snacks.
2. **Weather Awareness**: Portugal's weather can be unpredictable, so check forecasts and dress in layers.
3. **Maps and Guides**: Some trails may not be well-marked; consider downloading maps or hiring a local guide for longer hikes.
4. **Respect Nature**: Stick to designated paths, avoid littering, and respect local wildlife.
5. **Safety First**: Inform someone of your plans, especially for remote trails, and carry a charged phone with emergency contacts.

Whether you're marveling at the dramatic cliffs of Cabo da Roca, exploring the serene forests of Gerês, or wandering through the vineyards of Douro Valley, Portugal's hiking trails and nature escapes offer unforgettable experiences for every outdoor enthusiast.

Wine Tours and Tastings

Portugal's wine culture is world-renowned, and Porto and Lisbon are perfect starting points for discovering the country's rich winemaking heritage. From the famous Port wines of the Douro Valley to the crisp whites of Vinho Verde and robust reds of Alentejo, there's a wine to suit every palate. Explore these regions through guided tours and tastings, and immerse yourself in the art of winemaking.

Wine Tours and Tastings Near Porto

1. Douro Valley

- **Why Visit**: A UNESCO World Heritage site, the Douro Valley is the birthplace of Port wine, featuring terraced vineyards and stunning river views.
- **Top Experiences**:
    - **Quinta do Crasto**: Known for its award-winning wines and infinity pool overlooking the valley.
    - **Quinta da Pacheca**: Offers wine tastings and the unique option of staying in wine barrel-shaped accommodations.
    - **Boat Cruises**: Combine your wine tour with a scenic Douro River cruise.
- **How to Get There**: 1.5–2 hours by car or train from Porto.
- **Highlights**: Guided tastings, traditional wine-making methods, and scenic landscapes.

2. Vila Nova de Gaia Wine Cellars

- **Why Visit**: Located just across the river from Porto, this area is home to the historic Port wine cellars.
- **Top Experiences**:
    - **Taylor's Port Cellar**: Offers a comprehensive tour and tasting experience, with a terrace overlooking Porto.
    - **Graham's Lodge**: Known for its premium Ports and panoramic views.
    - **Cálem Cellars**: Features multimedia exhibits and fado music performances.
- **How to Get There**: A short walk or metro ride from central Porto.
- **Highlights**: Convenient location, immersive cellar tours, and diverse Port varieties.

3. Vinho Verde Region

- **Why Visit**: Known for its light, refreshing wines, perfect for summer sipping.
- **Top Experiences**:
    - **Quinta da Aveleda**: Famous for its Vinho Verde and stunning gardens.
    - **Quinta de Santa Cristina**: Offers guided vineyard tours and tastings.
- **How to Get There**: 1–1.5 hours by car from Porto.
- **Highlights**: Unique wine style, picturesque vineyards, and food pairings.

Wine Tours and Tastings Near Lisbon

1. Alentejo Wine Region

- **Why Visit**: Known for its robust reds and charming countryside, the Alentejo region offers a more rustic wine experience.
- **Top Experiences**:
    - **Herdade do Esporão**: A renowned estate with a variety of wine and olive oil tastings.
    - **Adega da Cartuxa**: Famous for its Pêra-Manca wines and historical setting.
- **How to Get There**: 1.5–2 hours by car from Lisbon.
- **Highlights**: Traditional wine-making methods, peaceful surroundings, and historic estates.

2. Setúbal Peninsula

- **Why Visit**: Famous for its sweet Moscatel wines and stunning coastal scenery.
- **Top Experiences**:
    - **José Maria da Fonseca**: One of Portugal's oldest wineries, known for its Moscatel and Periquita wines.
    - **Casa Museu José Maria da Fonseca**: Combines wine tastings with a museum tour.
- **How to Get There**: 45 minutes by car from Lisbon.
- **Highlights**: Sweet dessert wines, scenic coastal views, and historic estates.

3. Colares Wine Region

- **Why Visit**: Unique for its sandy soil vineyards and robust reds.
- **Top Experiences**:
    - **Adega Regional de Colares**: Offers tastings of wines made using traditional techniques.
    - **Vila de Colares**: Visit this quaint village for a more intimate wine experience.
- **How to Get There**: 30 minutes by car from Lisbon, near Sintra.
- **Highlights**: Rare wines, proximity to Lisbon, and historic vineyards.

4. Tejo Wine Region

- **Why Visit**: A lesser-known wine region with a long history and diverse wines.
- **Top Experiences**:
    - **Casa Cadaval**: A family-run estate offering guided tours and tastings.
    - **Quinta da Alorna**: Known for its premium wines and beautiful estate.
- **How to Get There**: 1 hour by car from Lisbon.
- **Highlights**: Affordable wines, intimate tastings, and scenic vineyards.

Tips for Wine Tours and Tastings

1. **Book in Advance**: Many wineries require reservations for tours and tastings, especially during peak seasons.
2. **Guided vs. Self-Guided**: Consider joining a guided wine tour for convenience or planning a self-guided trip for flexibility.
3. **Pair with Local Food**: Many wineries offer food pairings or even full meals—don't miss the chance to try local specialties.
4. **Transportation**: If you plan to drink, arrange for a driver or join a tour that includes transportation.
5. **Seasonal Considerations**: Visit during harvest season (September–October) for a chance to see winemaking in action.

Portugal's wine culture is more than just tasting—it's an opportunity to explore the country's landscapes, history, and traditions. Whether sipping a glass of Port along the Douro or discovering a hidden gem in Alentejo, these wine tours and tastings will leave you with a deeper appreciation for Portuguese wines.

Chapter 9: Food and Drink in Portugal

Traditional Portuguese Dishes

Portuguese cuisine is a delightful blend of Mediterranean flavors, fresh ingredients, and centuries-old recipes passed down through generations. From hearty stews and fresh seafood to sweet desserts, the country's culinary heritage reflects its history, geography, and maritime traditions. Below is a guide to must-try traditional dishes that highlight the diverse flavors of Portugal.

Seafood Specialties

1. Bacalhau à Brás

- **What It Is**: A popular dish made from shredded salted cod, onions, potatoes, and scrambled eggs, garnished with parsley and olives.
- **Why Try It**: Bacalhau (salt cod) is a staple of Portuguese cuisine, with over 365 variations to explore.

2. Grilled Sardines (Sardinhas Assadas)

- **What It Is**: Fresh sardines, simply seasoned with salt and grilled to perfection.
- **Why Try It**: A summer favorite, especially during Lisbon's Festas de Santo António in June.

3. Octopus Rice (Arroz de Polvo)

- **What It Is**: A rich and flavorful dish of tender octopus cooked with rice, tomatoes, and aromatic herbs.
- **Why Try It**: Combines Portugal's love of rice dishes with its abundant seafood.

4. Cataplana de Marisco

- **What It Is**: A seafood stew cooked in a traditional copper pot called a cataplana, featuring clams, shrimp, and fish in a fragrant tomato-based broth.
- **Why Try It**: Originating from the Algarve, it's a feast for seafood lovers.

Meat and Poultry Dishes

5. Cozido à Portuguesa

- **What It Is**: A hearty boiled stew of various meats (beef, pork, chicken), sausages, and vegetables.
- **Why Try It**: A rustic dish that showcases the diversity of Portuguese meats and cooking techniques.

6. Leitão à Bairrada

- **What It Is**: Roasted suckling pig, traditionally seasoned with garlic, white wine, and bay leaves.
- **Why Try It**: A crispy, tender delicacy, especially popular in the Bairrada region.

7. Alheira de Mirandela

- **What It Is**: A smoked sausage made from bread and a mix of meats such as chicken or game, often served fried with a fried egg and fries.
- **Why Try It**: A unique sausage with origins tied to Portugal's Jewish community.

Vegetarian-Friendly Dishes

8. Caldo Verde

- **What It Is**: A comforting soup made with kale, potatoes, and chouriço sausage (optional for vegetarians).
- **Why Try It**: A staple at Portuguese celebrations and perfect for a chilly evening.

9. Açorda

- **What It Is**: A bread-based dish flavored with garlic, cilantro, and olive oil, sometimes topped with poached eggs or shrimp.
- **Why Try It**: A simple yet flavorful dish showcasing traditional Portuguese ingredients.

Sweet Treats and Desserts

10. Pastéis de Nata

- **What It Is**: Iconic custard tarts with a flaky, buttery crust, dusted with cinnamon and powdered sugar.
- **Why Try It**: These world-famous pastries originated at the Jerónimos Monastery in Lisbon.

11. Queijadas

- **What It Is**: Small, sweet cheese tarts made from fresh cheese, eggs, and sugar.
- **Why Try It**: A traditional dessert from Sintra, perfect with a cup of coffee.

12. Arroz Doce

- **What It Is**: Portuguese rice pudding flavored with lemon zest and cinnamon.
- **Why Try It**: A comforting, home-style dessert found in many family kitchens.

13. Bolo de Bolacha

- **What It Is**: A layered cake made with Maria biscuits and a coffee-flavored cream.
- **Why Try It**: A no-bake treat that's both rich and nostalgic.

Bread and Snacks

14. Bifana

- **What It Is**: A sandwich of thinly sliced marinated pork served on a crusty bread roll.
- **Why Try It**: A simple, flavorful street food found at local tasquinhas (small eateries).

15. Pão de Deus

- **What It Is**: A sweet bread roll topped with coconut and sugar.
- **Why Try It**: Perfect as a breakfast treat or an afternoon snack with coffee.

16. Bolinhos de Bacalhau (Codfish Cakes)

- **What It Is**: Crispy, golden fritters made from salted cod, potatoes, and parsley.
- **Why Try It**: A beloved appetizer or snack served across Portugal.

Wine Pairing Tips

Portugal's cuisine pairs beautifully with its wines. Enjoy **Vinho Verde** with seafood, **Douro Reds** with meat dishes, and a glass of **Port** with desserts like Pastéis de Nata.

Exploring Portuguese cuisine is a journey into the heart of the country's culture and traditions. Whether you're savoring grilled sardines by the river or indulging in a pastel de nata at a Lisbon café, these dishes promise to make your trip unforgettable.

The Best Pastel de Nata Spots

No trip to Portugal is complete without indulging in the country's iconic custard tart: **pastel de nata**. With its golden, flaky crust and creamy custard filling, this beloved pastry is a must-try for locals and travelers alike. While you can find pastel de nata in almost any café in Portugal, these are the top spots renowned for their exceptional versions of this treat.

Top Pastel de Nata Spots in Lisbon

1. Pastéis de Belém

- **Why Go**: The original creators of the pastel de nata, dating back to 1837. Their recipe is a closely guarded secret, and their tarts are known for their unique, slightly caramelized custard and flaky crust.
- **Location**: Rua de Belém 84-92, Lisbon.
- **Price**: €1.30 per tart.
- **Tips**: Arrive early to avoid long queues, or opt for takeaway if the seating area is busy.

2. Manteigaria

- **Why Go**: Known for consistently fresh pastéis de nata, baked throughout the day. Each tart is served warm, with just the right balance of sweetness and crispiness.
- **Location**: Rua do Loreto 2, Lisbon (and other locations).
- **Price**: €1.20 per tart.
- **Tips**: Watch the bakers in action through the glass window while enjoying your treat.

3. Fabrica da Nata

- **Why Go**: Offers a modern twist on the classic pastel de nata, with options for pairing it with ice cream or espresso.
- **Location**: Praça dos Restauradores 62, Lisbon.
- **Price**: €1.20 per tart.
- **Tips**: Try their combo deals for a tart and coffee at an affordable price.

4. Aloma

- **Why Go**: Winner of multiple awards for its pastéis de nata, Aloma's version is buttery, creamy, and slightly less sweet than other versions.
- **Location**: Rua Francisco Metrass 67, Lisbon.
- **Price**: €1.15 per tart.
- **Tips**: Ideal for those who prefer a lighter custard.

Top Pastel de Nata Spots in Porto

1. Confeitaria do Bolhão

- **Why Go**: One of Porto's oldest bakeries, this spot serves traditional pastéis de nata with a rich custard and crispy shell.
- **Location**: Rua Formosa 339, Porto.
- **Price**: €1 per tart.
- **Tips**: Pair your tart with a galao (milky coffee) for an authentic Portuguese breakfast.

2. Nata Lisboa

- **Why Go**: A modern chain dedicated entirely to perfecting the pastel de nata. Their tarts are creamy and satisfying, with an emphasis on consistency.
- **Location**: Rua Santa Catarina 499, Porto (and other locations).
- **Price**: €1.20 per tart.
- **Tips**: Ideal for travelers who want to grab a quick bite on the go.

3. Fábrica de Nata Porto

- **Why Go**: The Porto branch of this famous Lisbon bakery serves freshly baked, golden-brown pastéis de nata in a cozy, inviting atmosphere.
- **Location**: Rua de Santa Catarina 331, Porto.
- **Price**: €1.20 per tart.
- **Tips**: Enjoy your tart with their aromatic Portuguese espresso.

4. Leitaria da Quinta do Paço

- **Why Go**: While known for its éclairs, this bakery also produces excellent pastéis de nata with a unique homemade touch.
- **Location**: Praça Guilherme Gomes Fernandes 47, Porto.
- **Price**: €1.50 per tart.
- **Tips**: If you're feeling adventurous, try both their éclairs and pastéis de nata.

Tips for the Perfect Pastel de Nata Experience

1. **Enjoy It Warm**: Pastéis de nata are best enjoyed fresh out of the oven, when the custard is warm, and the crust is crisp.
2. **Add a Sprinkle of Cinnamon or Sugar**: Many locals top their tarts with a light dusting of powdered cinnamon or sugar for extra flavor.
3. **Pair with Coffee**: Order a bica (Portuguese espresso) or a galao to enhance the experience.
4. **Try More Than One**: Each bakery has its own twist on the recipe, so sampling a few is a great way to discover your favorite.

Portugal's pastéis de nata are more than just a dessert—they're a taste of the country's rich culinary heritage. Whether in Lisbon, Porto, or a hidden café in between, each tart promises a bite of perfection.

Iconic Wines and Ports in Portugal

Portugal is a wine lover's paradise, boasting a rich winemaking tradition that spans centuries. The country is renowned for its diverse wine regions, unique grape varieties, and exceptional fortified wines, particularly Port. From the rolling vineyards of the Douro Valley to the crisp whites of Vinho Verde, Portugal's wines are as varied as its landscapes. Here's a guide to some of the most iconic Portuguese wines and ports to explore during your visit.

Port Wine: Portugal's Fortified Gem

Port wine, or simply Port, is a sweet, fortified wine produced exclusively in the Douro Valley in northern Portugal. It is a global symbol of Portuguese winemaking excellence.

1. Ruby Port

- **What It Is**: A young, fruity port with vibrant red hues and flavors of ripe berries.
- **Best With**: Desserts like chocolate cake or fruit tarts.

2. Tawny Port

- **What It Is**: A port aged in wooden barrels, giving it a nutty, caramelized flavor with hints of dried fruit.
- **Best With**: Cheese, nuts, or crème brûlée.

3. Vintage Port

- **What It Is**: Made from the best grapes of a single vintage year, this port is rich, complex, and meant to age for decades.
- **Best With**: Special occasions and rich desserts.

4. White Port

- **What It Is**: A less common variety made from white grapes, with flavors ranging from dry and crisp to sweet and honeyed.
- **Best With**: Aperitifs or cocktails.

Douro Valley Reds

The Douro Valley, the birthplace of Port wine, is also home to some of Portugal's finest red wines. These robust, full-bodied wines are made from native grape varieties like Touriga Nacional, Tinta Roriz, and Touriga Franca.

1. Douro DOC Reds

- **What They Are**: Rich, structured wines with flavors of dark fruit, spice, and earthiness.
- **Best With**: Roasted meats or hearty stews.

2. Quinta Wines

- **What They Are**: Wines produced by individual estates (quintas), often reflecting the unique terroir of each vineyard.
- **Best With**: Fine dining or wine tasting events.

Vinho Verde: Crisp and Refreshing

1. Vinho Verde White

- **What It Is**: A young, slightly effervescent white wine with bright acidity and citrus notes.
- **Best With**: Fresh seafood, salads, or light appetizers.

2. Vinho Verde Rosé

- **What It Is**: A pink-hued wine with fruity, floral aromas and a refreshing finish.
- **Best With**: Tapas or summer picnics.

3. Vinho Verde Red

- **What It Is**: A lesser-known style made from red grapes, offering vibrant acidity and light tannins.
- **Best With**: Traditional Portuguese dishes like roasted cod.

Alentejo: The Warm Heart of Portuguese Wine

The Alentejo region produces some of Portugal's most approachable and easy-drinking wines, both red and white.

1. Alentejo Reds

- **What They Are**: Smooth, full-bodied wines with flavors of ripe fruit, vanilla, and spice.
- **Best With**: Grilled meats or traditional stews.

2. Alentejo Whites

- **What They Are**: Aromatic, balanced wines with notes of tropical fruit and floral hints.
- **Best With**: Chicken dishes or creamy cheeses.

Other Noteworthy Regions and Styles

1. Dão

- **What It Is**: A high-altitude region known for elegant reds with balanced acidity and mineral notes.
- **Best With**: Game meats or roasted vegetables.

2. Madeira Wine

- **What It Is**: A fortified wine from Madeira Island, with flavors ranging from dry and nutty to sweet and caramelized.
- **Best With**: Desserts or as a cooking ingredient.

3. Bairrada

- **What It Is**: Famous for its sparkling wines and red wines made from the Baga grape.
- **Best With**: Suckling pig or fatty fish.

Wine Tasting Tips in Portugal

1. **Visit a Quinta**: Many wine estates in the Douro Valley and beyond offer tours, tastings, and even accommodations.
2. **Explore Wine Bars**: Cities like Porto and Lisbon have a vibrant wine bar scene, offering curated selections of local wines.
3. **Pair with Local Food**: Portuguese wines shine when paired with the country's diverse cuisine, so experiment with different combinations.
4. **Learn the Labels**: Look for classifications like DOC (Denominação de Origem Controlada) for high-quality, region-specific wines.

Portugal's wines and ports are an integral part of its culture and history. Whether you're sipping a glass of Vinho Verde by the coast or enjoying a vintage Port after dinner, each sip tells a story of tradition, craftsmanship, and passion.

Chapter 10: Shopping and Souvenirs

Best Shopping Streets and Markets

Portugal's vibrant shopping scene offers everything from traditional crafts and antiques to high-end fashion and gourmet delicacies. In Porto and Lisbon, you'll find a mix of bustling markets, charming boutiques, and elegant shopping streets that cater to a variety of tastes and budgets. Whether you're hunting for souvenirs, local specialties, or luxury items, these destinations are sure to delight.

Shopping Streets in Lisbon

1. Avenida da Liberdade

- **What It Is**: Lisbon's premier shopping boulevard, known for its luxury boutiques, high-end fashion brands, and elegant ambiance.
- **What to Buy**: Designer clothing, jewelry, and upscale accessories from brands like Gucci, Louis Vuitton, and Prada.
- **Tips**: Even if you're not shopping, take a stroll along this beautiful tree-lined avenue and enjoy the intricate mosaic sidewalks.

2. Rua Augusta

- **What It Is**: A bustling pedestrian street in the heart of Lisbon's Baixa district, lined with shops, cafes, and street performers.
- **What to Buy**: Affordable fashion, accessories, and Portuguese souvenirs like azulejos (ceramic tiles) and cork products.
- **Tips**: Don't miss the iconic Rua Augusta Arch at the end of the street for stunning views of the city.

3. Chiado District

- **What It Is**: A trendy neighborhood blending historic charm with modern style, offering a mix of global brands and independent shops.
- **What to Buy**: Portuguese fashion labels, books, and gourmet chocolates.
- **Tips**: Visit Livraria Bertrand, the world's oldest operating bookstore, and indulge in coffee at Café A Brasileira.

Shopping Streets in Porto

1. Rua de Santa Catarina

- **What It Is**: Porto's main shopping street, packed with a mix of international chains, independent boutiques, and charming cafes.
- **What to Buy**: Clothing, footwear, and traditional souvenirs.
- **Tips**: Visit the ornate Café Majestic for a coffee break and explore Via Catarina Shopping Mall for more options.

2. Avenida dos Aliados

- **What It Is**: A grand avenue in the city center featuring shops, banks, and historic architecture.
- **What to Buy**: High-quality Portuguese brands and artisanal crafts.
- **Tips**: Enjoy the scenic surroundings as you shop, and look out for seasonal fairs and events.

3. Miguel Bombarda Street

- **What It Is**: Porto's creative hub, filled with art galleries, concept stores, and design-focused shops.
- **What to Buy**: Contemporary art, handmade jewelry, and unique home décor.
- **Tips**: Visit on Saturdays for the Bombarda Art District's gallery openings and street events.

Must-Visit Markets in Lisbon

1. Mercado da Ribeira (Time Out Market)

- **What It Is**: A modern food market offering gourmet food stalls, local delicacies, and a selection of Portuguese wines.
- **What to Buy**: Gourmet foods, local wines, and artisanal products.
- **Tips**: Enjoy a meal or snack from one of the renowned chefs' stalls after shopping.

2. Feira da Ladra

- **What It Is**: Lisbon's famous flea market, held every Tuesday and Saturday in the Alfama district.
- **What to Buy**: Vintage items, antiques, second-hand books, and unique trinkets.
- **Tips**: Arrive early for the best finds and be prepared to haggle.

3. Mercado de Campo de Ourique

- **What It Is**: A charming neighborhood market offering fresh produce, specialty foods, and trendy eateries.
- **What to Buy**: Gourmet olive oils, cheeses, and pastries.
- **Tips**: Combine shopping with a meal at one of the market's many food stalls.

Must-Visit Markets in Porto

1. Mercado do Bolhão

- **What It Is**: Porto's iconic market, known for its vibrant atmosphere and fresh produce.
- **What to Buy**: Fresh fruits, vegetables, fish, and traditional Portuguese snacks.
- **Tips**: Explore both the food stalls and the small shops selling souvenirs and crafts.

2. Mercado Porto Belo

- **What It Is**: A weekend flea market held in the historic Praça de Carlos Alberto.
- **What to Buy**: Vintage clothing, vinyl records, handmade goods, and antiques.
- **Tips**: Ideal for finding unique and affordable souvenirs.

3. Mercado Ferreira Borges

- **What It Is**: A 19th-century iron market building now housing shops, restaurants, and cultural events.
- **What to Buy**: Contemporary Portuguese designs and specialty foods.
- **Tips**: Visit in the evening to enjoy the lively bar and entertainment scene.

Tips for Shopping in Portugal

1. **Look for Authentic Products**: Keep an eye out for local specialties like cork products, azulejos (tiles), handmade ceramics, and Portuguese textiles.
2. **Timing Matters**: Markets are best visited early for fresh produce and unique finds, while stores often have seasonal sales in January and July.
3. **Tax-Free Shopping**: Non-EU visitors can claim a VAT refund on purchases over €50. Ask for a tax-free form when shopping.
4. **Support Local Artisans**: Visit independent shops and markets to discover unique, handmade products that support local communities.

Shopping in Lisbon and Porto isn't just about purchasing goods; it's about immersing yourself in the vibrant culture and creativity of Portugal. From lively markets to elegant boulevards, you're sure to find treasures that make your trip unforgettable.

Unique Portuguese Handicrafts

Portugal is a treasure trove of artisanal traditions, with each region offering unique handicrafts that reflect its culture, history, and artistry. From intricate ceramics to finely woven textiles, these crafts make for perfect souvenirs or gifts. Here's a guide to some of Portugal's most iconic handmade products and where to find them.

1. Azulejos (Hand-Painted Tiles)

- **What They Are**: Decorative ceramic tiles, often hand-painted with intricate patterns, scenes from history, or geometric designs.
- **Origin**: Introduced during Moorish rule and now an integral part of Portuguese architecture.
- **What to Look For**: Authentic hand-painted azulejos with traditional blue-and-white or multicolored designs.
- **Where to Find Them**:
    - Lisbon: The National Tile Museum (Museu Nacional do Azulejo) offers both history and curated selections.
    - Porto: Independent shops in the Ribeira district or the Mercado do Bolhão.

2. Cork Products

- **What They Are**: Items made from cork, a sustainable material harvested from cork oak trees, which thrive in Portugal.
- **What to Look For**: Wallets, bags, hats, shoes, coasters, and even jewelry.
- **Where to Find Them**:
    - Lisbon: A Vida Portuguesa in Chiado for high-quality cork products.
    - Across Portugal: Shops specializing in eco-friendly gifts.

---

3. Embroidery and Lace

- **What It Is**: Fine embroidery and lacework, often handmade using techniques passed down through generations.
- **Notable Styles**:
    - Viana do Castelo: Known for vibrant, colorful embroidery with floral and heart motifs.
    - Madeira: Famous for delicate, intricate lacework.
- **Where to Find Them**:
    - Porto: Mercado do Bolhão and artisan shops in the city center.
    - Madeira: Specialty stores and markets on the island.

---

4. Arraiolos Rugs

- **What They Are**: Hand-embroidered wool rugs inspired by Persian carpet designs, originating from the town of Arraiolos in Alentejo.
- **What to Look For**: Rugs with vibrant geometric or floral patterns, created using traditional cross-stitch techniques.
- **Where to Find Them**:
    - Arraiolos: Workshops in the town itself.
    - Lisbon: Specialty stores like Arraiolos Carpet shops.

---

5. Filigree Jewelry

- **What It Is**: Delicate gold or silver jewelry crafted with fine threads, often shaped into intricate patterns like hearts or flowers.
- **What to Look For**:
    - Viana Hearts: A symbol of love and devotion, often seen in necklaces or earrings.
    - Earrings and pendants with traditional Portuguese motifs.
- **Where to Find Them**:
    - Northern Portugal: Cities like Gondomar and Viana do Castelo, home to master filigree artisans.

---

6. Pottery and Ceramics

- **What They Are**: Traditional pottery pieces, ranging from simple earthenware to colorful decorative items.
- **Notable Types**:
    - Barcelos Roosters: Colorful ceramic roosters, a symbol of good luck.
    - Alentejo Pottery: Rustic earthenware with floral or animal motifs.
- **Where to Find Them**:
    - Barcelos: Local markets and artisan workshops.
    - Alentejo: Towns like São Pedro do Corval, a hub for pottery.

---

7. Portuguese Knives

- **What They Are**: Handcrafted folding knives with wooden or horn handles, known for their quality and durability.
- **Notable Style**: The Palaçoulo knife, crafted in the Trás-os-Montes region.
- **Where to Find Them**:
    - Northern Portugal: Artisans in Palaçoulo.
    - Specialty knife shops across the country.

8. Portuguese Wool and Textiles

- **What They Are**: High-quality wool blankets, shawls, and clothing items made using traditional looms.
- **Notable Item**: Burel wool from Serra da Estrela, known for its warmth and durability.
- **Where to Find Them**:
    - Serra da Estrela: Workshops and stores in the region.
    - Lisbon: Burel Factory shop in the city.

---

9. Basket Weaving

- **What It Is**: Handmade baskets crafted from reeds or straw, often used for storage or decoration.
- **Notable Regions**:
    - Algarve: Known for colorful woven designs.
    - Minho: Specializes in sturdy, functional baskets.
- **Where to Find Them**:
    - Local markets throughout Portugal.

---

10. Traditional Portuguese Shoes

- **What They Are**: Handmade leather shoes and boots, crafted with care and attention to detail.
- **Notable Style**: The Portuguese clog (socas), once a staple of rural life.
- **Where to Find Them**:
    - Porto: Boutiques specializing in artisanal footwear.
    - Across Portugal: Leather shops and markets.

Tips for Buying Portuguese Handicrafts

1. **Check for Authenticity**: Opt for items labeled as handmade or locally produced.
2. **Shop Local Markets**: Markets like Feira da Ladra in Lisbon and Mercado do Bolhão in Porto often feature local artisans.
3. **Support Artisans**: Purchase directly from workshops or small businesses to support traditional craftsmanship.
4. **Pack Carefully**: If buying fragile items like ceramics, ensure they are securely packed for travel.

Portugal's rich heritage is beautifully captured in its handicrafts. Whether you're taking home an intricate azulejo tile or a warm wool blanket, each piece carries the story of Portugal's artistry and tradition.

Where to Buy Authentic Tiles and Ceramics

Portugal's tiles and ceramics are iconic, blending artistry and cultural heritage. Whether you're looking for traditional azulejos (hand-painted tiles) or contemporary ceramics, there are plenty of places across the country to find authentic, high-quality pieces. Here's a guide to where you can purchase these treasures:

1. Lisbon

A. National Tile Museum (Museu Nacional do Azulejo)

- **What It Offers**: A collection of historical tiles and a gift shop where you can buy replicas and authentic azulejos.
- **Why Visit**: Combines history with shopping, giving you context about the art form.
- **Location**: Rua da Madre de Deus, 4, Lisbon.

B. Sant'Anna Factory

- **What It Offers**: Handcrafted azulejos and ceramics made using traditional techniques.
- **Why Visit**: Established in 1741, this factory is renowned for its exquisite craftsmanship.
- **Location**: Calçada da Boa Hora, 96, Lisbon.

C. Cortiço & Netos

- **What It Offers**: Vintage tiles and unique designs, often sourced from old Portuguese buildings.
- **Why Visit**: Ideal for finding rare or discontinued tile patterns.
- **Location**: Avenida Almirante Reis, 123, Lisbon.

---

2. Porto

A. Mercado do Bolhão

- **What It Offers**: A variety of stalls selling traditional Portuguese products, including tiles and ceramics.
- **Why Visit**: A lively market atmosphere with options for affordable souvenirs.
- **Location**: Rua Formosa, Porto.

B. Cerâmicas Narciso

- **What It Offers**: Unique handmade tiles and ceramic products, showcasing contemporary and traditional styles.
- **Why Visit**: Combines modern aesthetics with Portuguese tile heritage.
- **Location**: Rua do Almada, 275, Porto.

C. Loja das Tábuas

- **What It Offers**: Beautifully crafted tiles and other handmade ceramics.
- **Why Visit**: Perfect for finding unique designs for home décor.
- **Location**: Rua de São João, 61, Porto.

---

3. Alentejo Region

A. São Pedro do Corval

- **What It Offers**: Known as Portugal's pottery capital, this village is home to numerous workshops.
- **Why Visit**: Watch artisans at work and purchase directly from the creators.
- **Location**: Near Reguengos de Monsaraz in the Alentejo region.

B. Oficina da Terra

- **What It Offers**: Traditional Alentejo-style ceramics with colorful and intricate patterns.
- **Why Visit**: Authentic designs that make for great gifts or décor items.
- **Location**: Évora, Alentejo.

---

4. Algarve Region

A. Porches Pottery

- **What It Offers**: Hand-painted ceramics, focusing on traditional Algarve designs.
- **Why Visit**: One of the Algarve's most famous pottery workshops.
- **Location**: EN125, Porches, Algarve.

B. Tavira Ceramics

- **What It Offers**: A blend of modern and traditional styles, reflecting the coastal charm of the Algarve.
- **Why Visit**: A great place to find unique ceramics that reflect the region's aesthetic.
- **Location**: Tavira, Algarve.

---

5. Online Stores

A. Made in Portugal Online

- **What It Offers**: A wide selection of handmade tiles and ceramics, available for international shipping.
- **Why Visit**: Ideal for purchasing authentic Portuguese products from anywhere in the world.
- **Website**: www.madeinportugal.com

B. A Vida Portuguesa

- **What It Offers**: Curated selections of Portuguese handicrafts, including azulejos and ceramics.
- **Why Visit**: Known for supporting local artisans and offering high-quality items.

- **Website**: www.avidaportuguesa.com

chapter 11: Seasonal Travel Tips

What to Expect in Each Season

Portugal's climate and charm shift with the seasons, offering unique experiences throughout the year. Whether you're visiting in the heat of summer or the crispness of winter, knowing what to expect in each season will help you make the most of your trip to Porto and Lisbon.

Spring (March to May)

Weather:

- Mild and pleasant, with temperatures ranging from 12°C to 20°C (54°F to 68°F).
- Occasional rainfall, especially in March, but overall sunny days become more frequent.

What to Expect:

- Blooming flowers and lush greenery make this a picturesque time to explore parks and gardens.
- Cultural events and festivals, such as Lisbon's IndieLisboa Film Festival in April.
- Fewer crowds compared to summer, making it ideal for sightseeing in cities and enjoying outdoor activities.

Highlights:

- Walk along the Douro River in Porto or relax in Lisbon's Eduardo VII Park.
- Visit the Sintra-Cascais Natural Park for stunning springtime landscapes.

Summer (June to August)

Weather:

- Hot and sunny, with temperatures ranging from 20°C to 30°C (68°F to 86°F) and higher in inland areas.

- Coastal breezes in Porto and Lisbon provide some relief from the heat.

What to Expect:

- Peak tourist season, with bustling streets, vibrant nightlife, and crowded attractions.
- Long daylight hours for sightseeing and late-night dinners.
- Numerous festivals, including Porto's São João Festival in June and Lisbon's Feast of St. Anthony.

Highlights:

- Enjoy the beaches near Lisbon, such as Cascais or Costa da Caparica.
- Take a wine tour in the Douro Valley or attend music festivals like NOS Alive in Lisbon.

Autumn (September to November)

Weather:

- Warm in early autumn, gradually cooling to temperatures between 15°C and 22°C (59°F to 72°F).
- Light rain showers become more common in November.

What to Expect:

- Harvest season brings wine festivals and culinary events, perfect for food and wine lovers.
- Quieter streets and attractions as the summer crowds fade.
- Beautiful fall foliage in parks and countryside areas.

Highlights:

- Visit Porto's Gaia district for port wine cellars and tastings.
- Explore Lisbon's Alfama neighborhood during golden autumn evenings.

Winter (December to February)

Weather:

- Cool but not freezing, with temperatures ranging from 8°C to 15°C (46°F to 59°F).
- Rain is more frequent, but there are still plenty of sunny days.

What to Expect:

- Off-season means fewer tourists, lower accommodation prices, and shorter lines at attractions.
- Festive holiday decorations and markets, particularly in December.
- Great time to experience Portugal's hearty winter cuisine, like cozido à portuguesa.

Highlights:

- Visit Porto's Livraria Lello or Lisbon's cafés for cozy indoor activities.
- Celebrate New Year's Eve at Praça do Comércio in Lisbon or Ribeira Square in Porto.

Seasonal Tips

1. **Spring and Autumn**: Pack layers for changing temperatures and light rain. Ideal for cultural exploration and outdoor activities.
2. **Summer**: Bring sunscreen, a hat, and breathable clothing. Book accommodations and attractions well in advance.
3. **Winter**: Dress warmly, especially for evenings. Use the quieter season to explore museums and indoor attractions.
4. **Festivals**: Check local calendars for seasonal festivals and events to enhance your travel experience.

Each season offers its own allure, from the lively summer streets to the tranquil charm of winter. No matter when you visit, Porto and Lisbon promise unforgettable experiences!

Seasonal Activities and Events

Portugal's rich cultural calendar offers something exciting every season, from lively festivals to unique seasonal experiences. Here's a breakdown of activities and events in Porto and Lisbon to help you plan your trip around the best the seasons have to offer.

Spring (March to May)

Activities:

- **Explore Gardens and Parks**: Spring blooms bring places like Lisbon's Jardim da Estrela and Porto's Jardins do Palácio de Cristal to life.
- **River Cruises**: Enjoy a scenic cruise along the Douro River as the countryside turns green and vibrant.
- **Hiking**: Take advantage of mild weather for hikes in Sintra-Cascais Natural Park or Serra da Arrábida.

Events:

- **IndieLisboa Film Festival (April)**: Lisbon's renowned independent film festival showcases international and Portuguese films.
- **Semana Santa (Holy Week, March/April)**: Religious parades and events take place in cities like Braga and Porto, offering a glimpse into Portuguese traditions.
- **Lisbon Book Fair (May)**: Held in Eduardo VII Park, this event is a book lover's dream with author signings and cultural talks.

Summer (June to August)

Activities:

- **Beach Days**: Relax at beaches near Lisbon (Cascais, Estoril) or Porto (Espinho, Matosinhos).
- **Wine Tasting**: Summer is perfect for vineyard tours in the Douro Valley or Setúbal region.
- **Outdoor Concerts**: Enjoy live music in plazas or open-air venues.

Events:

- **São João Festival (June 23-24)**: Porto comes alive with music, dancing, fireworks, and the quirky tradition of tapping people on the head with plastic hammers.
- **Feast of St. Anthony (June 12-13)**: Lisbon's Alfama district is filled with street parties, grilled sardines, and parades in honor of its patron saint.
- **NOS Alive Festival (July)**: One of Europe's top music festivals, held in Lisbon, featuring international and local artists.

Autumn (September to November)

Activities:

- **Wine Harvest Experiences**: Participate in grape stomping and wine-making tours in the Douro Valley.
- **Cultural Exploration**: Wander quieter streets and enjoy museums like the Calouste Gulbenkian Museum in Lisbon or Serralves Museum in Porto.
- **Food Tours**: Fall is the best time to sample seasonal dishes, like chestnuts and hearty stews.

Events:

- **Porto Wine Fest (September)**: Celebrate Porto's most famous export with tastings, food pairings, and workshops.
- **Lisbon Fashion Week (October)**: Showcasing top Portuguese designers, this event highlights Lisbon's growing influence in the fashion world.
- **St. Martin's Day (November 11)**: A traditional celebration marking the end of the harvest, featuring roasted chestnuts and local wines.

Winter (December to February)

Activities:

- **Holiday Shopping**: Stroll through Christmas markets like Mercado de Natal in Porto or Wonderland Lisboa.
- **Historic Tours**: Visit iconic landmarks like Jerónimos Monastery in Lisbon or Livraria Lello in Porto without the crowds.
- **Cozy Culinary Experiences**: Savor winter comfort foods like caldo verde (kale soup) and pastéis de nata with a glass of warm port wine.

Events:

- **Christmas Lights and Markets (December)**: Both cities are adorned with festive lights and decorations, offering a magical atmosphere.
- **New Year's Eve Celebrations (December 31)**: Fireworks light up Lisbon's Praça do Comércio and Porto's Ribeira district.
- **Fantasporto Film Festival (February)**: Porto's international fantasy and sci-fi film festival draws movie enthusiasts from around the world.

Year-Round Must-Dos

- **Fado Performances**: Enjoy traditional Portuguese music in cozy taverns or dedicated venues in both cities.
- **Culinary Workshops**: Learn to make iconic dishes like bacalhau à brás (codfish) or custard tarts.
- **Market Visits**: Explore Mercado do Bolhão in Porto or Mercado da Ribeira in Lisbon for fresh produce and local delicacies.

Tips for Attending Events and Activities

1. **Plan Ahead**: Popular events like São João or NOS Alive can sell out quickly—book tickets and accommodations early.
2. **Dress Appropriately**: Bring comfortable walking shoes for festivals and consider layers for cooler evenings.
3. **Immerse Yourself**: Don't just observe—participate! Whether it's dancing in the streets during São João or helping with the wine harvest, active involvement enriches your experience.

Weather and Packing Advice

Portugal enjoys a diverse climate, with warm summers, mild winters, and regional variations influenced by its coastal and inland geography. Knowing what to expect in terms of weather and what to pack will ensure you're prepared for your trip to Porto, Lisbon, and beyond.

Weather Overview by Season

Spring (March to May)

- **Temperatures**: 12°C to 20°C (54°F to 68°F).
- **Characteristics**: Mild and pleasant with occasional rain, especially in March. Blossoming flowers make this a scenic time to visit.
- **Packing Tips**:
    - Light layers: T-shirts, long-sleeve tops, and a lightweight jacket.
    - Comfortable walking shoes for city exploration and parks.
    - A compact umbrella or rain jacket for spring showers.

Summer (June to August)

- **Temperatures**: 20°C to 30°C (68°F to 86°F), occasionally higher inland.
- **Characteristics**: Hot and dry, with cooler evenings and coastal breezes. Long, sunny days perfect for outdoor activities.
- **Packing Tips**:
    - Breathable clothing: Light fabrics such as linen or cotton.
    - Sun protection: Sunglasses, a wide-brimmed hat, and sunscreen (SPF 30+).
    - Swimwear for beach visits.
    - Comfortable sandals or lightweight sneakers.

Autumn (September to November)

- **Temperatures**: 15°C to 22°C (59°F to 72°F), gradually cooling.
- **Characteristics**: Warm early autumn with cooler evenings; rainfall increases in November.
- **Packing Tips**:
    - Layered clothing: Short-sleeve shirts, sweaters, and a medium-weight jacket.
    - Waterproof footwear and an umbrella for occasional rain.

- A scarf or shawl for breezy evenings.

Winter (December to February)

- **Temperatures**: 8°C to 15°C (46°F to 59°F).
- **Characteristics**: Cool but not freezing, with rain more frequent than in other seasons. Lisbon tends to be slightly warmer than Porto.
- **Packing Tips**:
    - Warm layers: Sweaters, a warm coat, and long pants.
    - Waterproof shoes and a sturdy umbrella.
    - Gloves and a scarf for chillier days, especially in northern areas like Porto.

Packing Essentials for All Seasons

1. **Comfortable Shoes**: Both Porto and Lisbon have cobblestone streets and steep hills, so durable, non-slip footwear is a must.
2. **Daypack or Tote Bag**: Perfect for carrying water, snacks, and other essentials during city exploration or day trips.
3. **Adapters and Chargers**: Portugal uses type C and F power sockets (Europlug) with a standard voltage of 230V. Bring an adapter if needed.
4. **Reusable Water Bottle**: Stay hydrated while reducing plastic waste. Tap water is safe to drink in Portugal.
5. **Camera or Smartphone**: Capture the stunning architecture, vibrant neighborhoods, and scenic views.
6. **Medications and Toiletries**: Bring prescription medications and travel-sized toiletries, as some brands may not be readily available.
7. **Guidebook or Offline Maps**: For navigating areas where mobile coverage might be weak.

Season-Specific Packing Tips

Beach Trips (Summer)

- Beach towel and flip-flops.
- Waterproof phone pouch.
- Snorkeling gear (optional, as rentals are available).

Rainy Days (Spring/Autumn/Winter)

- A compact, wind-resistant umbrella.
- Waterproof outerwear like a trench coat or rain jacket.

Chilly Evenings (Winter)

- Thermal layers if you plan to visit northern regions or higher altitudes.
- A packable down jacket for extra warmth.

Weather App Recommendations

To stay informed about changing weather conditions, consider downloading reliable weather apps like:

- AccuWeather
- Weather.com
- Meteo.pt (Portugal-specific weather updates).

Packing strategically based on the season and activities ensures a comfortable and enjoyable experience in Portugal's dynamic climate. Whether you're walking along Lisbon's sunny streets or savoring a port wine in a cozy Porto café on a rainy day, you'll be prepared!

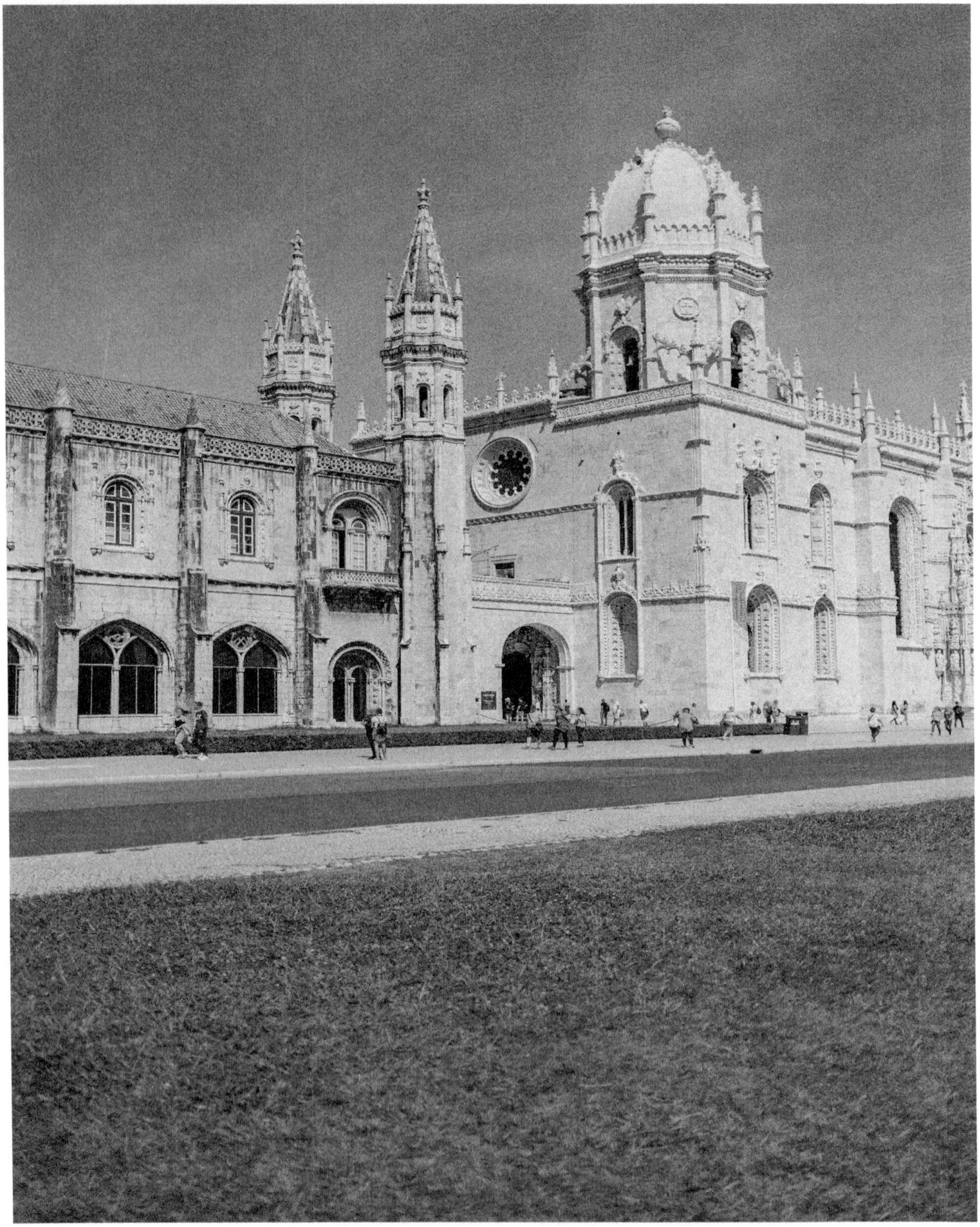

Chapter 12: Safety and Practical Information in Portugal

Health and Safety Tips

Your well-being is a priority when traveling, and Portugal, including the cities of Porto and Lisbon, is considered a safe and traveler-friendly destination. However, taking some precautions and staying informed ensures a stress-free trip. Here's a comprehensive guide to health and safety tips while visiting Portugal.

Health Tips

1. Travel Insurance

- Ensure you have comprehensive travel insurance that covers medical expenses, trip cancellations, and personal belongings.
- Check if your policy includes coverage for COVID-19-related medical care and travel disruptions.

2. Vaccinations and Medications

- No mandatory vaccinations are required to enter Portugal, but it's advisable to have routine vaccines like tetanus and hepatitis A up to date.
- Carry any prescription medications you may need, along with a copy of the prescription in case you need refills.
- Bring a small first-aid kit with essentials like band-aids, pain relievers, anti-diarrheal medicine, and motion sickness tablets.

3. Water and Food Safety

- Tap water in Portugal is safe to drink. Carry a reusable water bottle to stay hydrated.
- Food hygiene standards are high, so feel free to enjoy local dishes and street food.
- If you have food allergies or dietary restrictions, learn key phrases in Portuguese to communicate your needs or carry a translated allergy card.

4. Emergency Numbers

- The general emergency number in Portugal is **112**.
- Pharmacies (identified by a green cross) are well-stocked and staffed by knowledgeable professionals for minor medical issues.

Safety Tips

1. Personal Safety

- Portugal has low crime rates, but pickpocketing and petty theft can occur, particularly in tourist-heavy areas like Lisbon's Alfama district or Porto's Ribeira.
- Keep valuables close and use anti-theft bags or pouches.
- Avoid displaying large amounts of cash or expensive jewelry.

2. Transportation Safety

- Public transportation, including trams, buses, and trains, is generally safe. Be mindful of your belongings, especially on crowded trams like Lisbon's Tram 28.
- Use licensed taxis or ride-hailing apps like Bolt and Uber for reliable transportation.
- If renting a car, familiarize yourself with local driving laws and park in secure, well-lit areas.

3. Avoid Tourist Scams

- Be cautious of overly friendly strangers offering unsolicited help or services, especially near ATMs or ticket machines.
- Always use official ticket counters for attractions and public transport to avoid counterfeit tickets.

4. Natural Hazards

- Beaches: Pay attention to flags indicating water conditions. Red flags mean no swimming, and yellow means caution.
- Hiking: Stick to marked trails and wear appropriate footwear.
- Weather: In summer, apply sunscreen regularly and stay hydrated to prevent heatstroke. In winter, be prepared for sudden rainfall, especially in northern Portugal.

COVID-19 and Public Health Guidelines

- Stay updated on Portugal's latest COVID-19 travel regulations and entry requirements.
- Practice good hygiene by washing your hands regularly and using hand sanitizer.
- Masks may still be required in some medical settings; carry one just in case.

Women and Solo Travelers

- Portugal is generally safe for solo travelers, including women.
- Stick to well-lit, populated areas at night and inform someone of your itinerary when heading to remote areas.

Important Portuguese Phrases for Emergencies

1. **"Ajuda, por favor!"** – Help, please!
2. **"Chame uma ambulância!"** – Call an ambulance!
3. **"Onde fica a farmácia mais próxima?"** – Where is the nearest pharmacy?
4. **"Estou perdido/a."** – I am lost.

Travel Smart Tips

1. **Know Your Surroundings**: Always have a map or a navigation app handy. Offline maps like Google Maps or Maps.me are helpful.
2. **Respect Local Customs**: Understanding Portuguese etiquette, like waiting for everyone to be served before eating, ensures respectful interactions.
3. **Trust Your Instincts**: If something doesn't feel right, leave the area or seek assistance.

Portugal's welcoming culture, excellent healthcare facilities, and safe environment make it a delightful destination. By staying prepared and vigilant, you can enjoy your trip with confidence and peace of mind!

Emergency Contacts and Services

Being prepared for emergencies is an important part of travel. Portugal has a well-developed infrastructure to assist locals and visitors in urgent situations. Here is a comprehensive guide to emergency contacts and services in Porto, Lisbon, and other parts of Portugal.

General Emergency Number

- **112**: The universal emergency number in Portugal. It connects you to police, ambulance, fire services, and rescue operations.

Medical Emergencies

- **Ambulance Services**: Dial **112** for immediate medical assistance.

- **Hospitals**: Both Lisbon and Porto have modern hospitals with emergency departments. Some of the main hospitals include:

    - **Hospital de Santa Maria** (Lisbon): +351 217 805 000
    - **Hospital São João** (Porto): +351 225 512 100
- **Pharmacies**: Pharmacies (called "Farmácias") are easy to find in urban areas. They are marked with a green cross. For after-hours service, look for the nearest 24-hour pharmacy by checking the notice posted at any pharmacy door or by visiting the website **www.farmaciasdeservico.net**.

Police Services

- **General Police Assistance**: Dial **112**.
- **Tourism Police (Lisbon)**: +351 213 421 634
    - Special unit for assisting tourists in Lisbon, particularly in cases of theft or loss of documents.
- **PSP (Public Security Police)**: For non-emergency police assistance, visit a local station.

Fire Department

- **112**: Also connects to the fire department for emergencies such as fires, rescues, or hazardous situations.

Embassies and Consulates

If you lose your passport or require assistance from your home country, contact your nearest embassy or consulate. Here are some key contacts in Lisbon:

- **United States Embassy**: +351 217 273 300
- **United Kingdom Embassy**: +351 213 924 000
- **Canadian Embassy (in Paris, for Portugal)**: +33 1 44 43 29 00 (Portugal consular services are covered by the Paris office).

Lost or Stolen Documents

- Report stolen passports or identification immediately to the local police and your embassy.
- Request a police report to present to your embassy or consulate for emergency travel documents.

Transportation Assistance

- **Metro Services**:
    - Lisbon: +351 213 500 115 (Customer Support)
    - Porto: +351 225 081 000 (Andante hotline)
- **Taxis and Ride-Sharing**: Use official taxi services or apps like Bolt and Uber for safe transportation.

Tourist Support

- **Portugal Tourism Hotline (Linha de Apoio ao Turista)**: +351 808 209 209
    - Assistance for tourists, including travel advice, help with lost belongings, and information about local attractions.

Language Support

If you don't speak Portuguese, most emergency services operators have English-speaking staff. For additional help:

- Use translation apps like Google Translate for communicating in Portuguese.
- Learn a few key phrases:
    - **"Ajuda, por favor!"** – Help, please!
    - **"Chame uma ambulância!"** – Call an ambulance!
    - **"Fui roubado/a."** – I was robbed.
    - **"Perdi o meu passaporte."** – I lost my passport.

Roadside Assistance

For car breakdowns or accidents:

- **ACP (Automóvel Club de Portugal)**: +351 707 509 510
- **Brisa (Highway Assistance)**: +351 800 508 508

Hotline for Women and Vulnerable Travelers

- **APAV (Portuguese Association for Victim Support)**: +351 707 200 077
    - Assists victims of crime or abuse, including tourists.

Crisis and Mental Health Support

- **SOS Voz Amiga**: +351 800 202 669
    - A confidential helpline for anyone feeling overwhelmed or needing someone to talk to.

Mobile Apps for Emergencies

1. **112 Portugal**: An app that provides quick access to emergency services and allows location sharing.
2. **Google Maps**: To navigate to the nearest hospital, police station, or pharmacy.

3. **Red Cross First Aid App**: Offers step-by-step instructions for handling medical emergencies.

Having these contacts at hand ensures you're prepared to handle unexpected situations efficiently, making your trip to Porto, Lisbon, and other parts of Portugal as safe and stress-free as possible.

Staying Connected (Wi-Fi, SIM Cards)

Staying connected while traveling in Portugal is essential for navigating cities, staying in touch with loved ones, and sharing your experiences online. Here's a guide to ensure you're always connected in Lisbon, Porto, and beyond.

Wi-Fi Availability

1. Public Wi-Fi

- **Free Wi-Fi in Cities**: Lisbon and Porto offer free Wi-Fi hotspots in public areas, including parks, squares, and transportation hubs. Look for networks labeled "Free Wi-Fi" or "Wi-Fi Lisboa."
- **Cafes and Restaurants**: Most cafes, restaurants, and bars provide free Wi-Fi. Simply ask staff for the password.
- **Libraries and Museums**: Many public libraries and cultural attractions offer free internet access for visitors.

2. Hotel Wi-Fi

- Almost all hotels, guesthouses, and hostels in Portugal offer free Wi-Fi, although connection speeds can vary. Boutique and higher-end accommodations typically have reliable internet service.

3. Airports

- Both Lisbon (Humberto Delgado Airport) and Porto (Francisco Sá Carneiro Airport) offer free Wi-Fi for travelers.

SIM Cards for Travelers

Using a local SIM card is one of the most cost-effective ways to stay connected during your trip. Here's how to get started:

1. Major Providers

Portugal's primary mobile network providers are:

- **MEO**
- **Vodafone Portugal**
- **NOS**

All three providers have excellent coverage across Portugal, including rural and coastal areas.

2. Where to Buy a SIM Card

- **Airports**: SIM cards are available at kiosks and vending machines in Lisbon and Porto airports.
- **Shops and Retail Stores**: Visit official stores of MEO, Vodafone, or NOS in city centers or malls.
- **Convenience Stores**: Many supermarkets and smaller convenience stores sell prepaid SIM cards.

3. Prepaid SIM Plans

- Prices start at around €10-€20 for a prepaid SIM card, including data, calls, and texts.
- Plans often include 5GB-15GB of data, which is sufficient for most travelers.
- Unlimited social media data is included in some plans (e.g., Vodafone's tourist package).
- Recharge cards are available at retail stores or online.

4. Documents Required

- Bring your passport or an ID to purchase and activate a SIM card.

eSIM Options

For travelers with eSIM-compatible devices, you can activate a Portuguese mobile plan without needing a physical SIM card. Some popular eSIM providers include:

- **Airalo**: Offers affordable data plans tailored for Portugal or Europe.
- **Nomad**: Provides flexible plans with easy activation.

eSIMs are convenient and can be activated before you arrive, saving time at the airport or in the city.

Portable Wi-Fi Devices

If you need to connect multiple devices or prefer not to switch SIM cards, renting a portable Wi-Fi hotspot is a great alternative.

- **How It Works**: Portable hotspots create a personal Wi-Fi network that you can use with your phone, laptop, and other devices.
- **Rental Options**: Companies like Tep Wireless, Skyroam, and local providers offer daily or weekly rental plans.
- **Cost**: Around €6-€10 per day, depending on the provider and data allowance.

Roaming Options

If you're from an EU country:

- Portugal is part of the EU, so travelers from EU/EEA countries can use their home SIM cards without additional roaming charges under the "Roam Like at Home" policy.

If you're from outside the EU:

- Check with your provider about international roaming packages. These can be more expensive than purchasing a local SIM card.

Tips for Staying Connected

1. **Download Offline Maps**: Apps like Google Maps and Maps.me allow you to navigate even without an internet connection.
2. **Use Messaging Apps**: Free apps like WhatsApp, Facebook Messenger, and Viber are widely used in Portugal.
3. **Check Data Limits**: Keep an eye on your data usage, especially if your plan does not include unlimited data.
4. **Secure Your Connection**: Use a VPN when connecting to public Wi-Fi networks for added security.

Recommended Tourist SIM Card Plans

Vodafone Portugal

- **Plan**: €20 for 10GB of data, 500 minutes of local calls, and unlimited texts.
- **Validity**: 30 days.
- **Where to Buy**: Vodafone stores, airports, or online.

MEO

- **Plan**: €15 for 7GB of data and local calls.
- **Validity**: 15 days.
- **Where to Buy**: MEO stores and retail outlets.

NOS

- **Plan**: €10 for 5GB of data, with optional add-ons for calls and texts.
- **Validity**: 10 days.
- **Where to Buy**: NOS stores or convenience shops.

Staying connected in Portugal is easy and affordable with the right preparation. Whether you rely on public Wi-Fi, a local SIM card, or an eSIM, you'll have no trouble accessing maps, keeping in touch, or sharing your travel memories.

Chapter 13: Itineraries and Recommendations

3-Day Itinerary for First-Time Visitors

Whether you're exploring Portugal for the first time or looking for the perfect blend of history, culture, and gastronomy, this 3-day itinerary covers the highlights of Porto and Lisbon. Designed for a quick yet fulfilling trip, this plan ensures you experience the essence of these iconic cities.

Day 1: Porto – The Charms of the North

Morning

- **Ribeira District**: Start your day in Porto's vibrant riverside neighborhood, a UNESCO World Heritage site. Stroll along the cobbled streets and admire colorful buildings overlooking the Douro River.
- **São Bento Railway Station**: Stop to see the stunning azulejo (blue tile) murals depicting Portugal's history.
- **Livraria Lello**: Visit one of the world's most beautiful bookstores, rumored to have inspired J.K. Rowling.

Lunch

- **Café Santiago**: Indulge in Porto's iconic dish, the *Francesinha* sandwich, a hearty and cheesy meal perfect for refueling.

Afternoon

- **Clérigos Tower**: Climb the 240 steps for panoramic views of Porto's rooftops and the Douro River.
- **Bolsa Palace (Palácio da Bolsa)**: Take a guided tour of this 19th-century building and marvel at the stunning Arabian Hall.

Evening

- **Port Wine Cellars**: Cross the Dom Luís I Bridge to Vila Nova de Gaia and enjoy a guided port wine tasting at famous cellars like Graham's or Sandeman.
- **Dinner**: Dine riverside at **Taberna de Santo António**, known for authentic Portuguese dishes.

Day 2: Lisbon – History and Heritage

Morning

- Take an early train or flight to Lisbon (approximately 2.5 hours by train or 1 hour by flight).
- **Belém District**: Start at the **Belém Tower**, a 16th-century fortress and UNESCO site, and visit the **Monastery of Jerónimos** to see its intricate Manueline architecture.
- **Pastéis de Belém**: Treat yourself to the famous custard tarts at this legendary bakery.

Lunch

- Enjoy seafood at **Solar dos Presuntos**, renowned for its grilled fish and Portuguese classics.

Afternoon

- **Praça do Comércio**: Wander through Lisbon's grand riverside square and explore the shops and cafes.
- **Alfama District**: Stroll through Lisbon's oldest neighborhood, known for its narrow alleys, colorful houses, and local charm. Don't miss a visit to **Lisbon Cathedral (Sé de Lisboa)**.
- **Tram 28 Ride**: Hop on this iconic tram for a scenic journey through the city's historic areas.

Evening

- **Fado Dinner Experience**: Immerse yourself in Portuguese culture with a live Fado music performance at **Clube de Fado** or **A Baiuca**.

Day 3: Exploring Both Cities

Morning in Lisbon

- **Castle of São Jorge**: Begin your day with a visit to this medieval castle, offering breathtaking views over Lisbon and the Tagus River.
- **LX Factory**: A creative hub filled with shops, art studios, and quirky cafes, perfect for a late breakfast or brunch.

Travel to Porto

- Return to Porto by early afternoon (via train or flight).

Afternoon in Porto

- **Douro River Cruise**: Relax with a traditional rabelo boat tour on the Douro River. Admire the city's iconic bridges and stunning views from the water.
- **Crystal Palace Gardens**: Take a leisurely stroll in these picturesque gardens, enjoying panoramic views of Porto and the Douro Valley.

Evening

- **Farewell Dinner**: End your trip at **The Yeatman Restaurant**, a Michelin-starred dining experience with exceptional views of Porto's skyline.

Additional Tips

- **Transportation**: Both cities have excellent public transportation systems, including metros, trams, and buses. Use travel cards like the Andante Card in Porto and the Viva Viagem card in Lisbon for convenience.
- **Packing**: Comfortable walking shoes are essential for navigating cobbled streets and hilly terrain in both cities.
- **Timing**: Adjust the itinerary to your pace, skipping or adding activities based on your preferences.

This 3-day itinerary offers a perfect blend of cultural landmarks, culinary experiences, and memorable adventures, leaving you with a true appreciation of Portugal's most iconic cities.

One Week in Porto and Lisbon

Discover the best of Porto and Lisbon in one week with this carefully crafted itinerary. Experience the charm of these iconic cities, indulge in Portuguese cuisine, and explore nearby treasures with day trips. This guide balances cultural highlights, relaxation, and memorable activities.

Day 1: Arrival in Porto

Afternoon

- **Check-In and Relax**: Settle into your hotel or accommodation. Choose a central location near Ribeira or the Clérigos Tower for easy access to attractions.
- **Ribeira District**: Take a leisurely stroll along the Douro River. Enjoy the lively atmosphere, street performers, and views of the Dom Luís I Bridge.

Evening

- **Dinner**: Dine at **Casa Guedes**, famous for its pork sandwiches (*sandes de pernil*).
- **Sunset Viewpoint**: Walk across the Dom Luís I Bridge and enjoy the sunset from the Serra do Pilar Monastery.

Day 2: Exploring Porto

Morning

- **Livraria Lello**: Start your day at this iconic bookstore, known for its stunning interiors. Arrive early to avoid crowds.
- **São Bento Railway Station**: Admire the breathtaking azulejo tilework depicting Portugal's history.

Afternoon

- **Clérigos Tower**: Climb the tower for panoramic views of the city.
- **Bolhão Market**: Explore this bustling market to sample local delicacies or pick up unique souvenirs.

Evening

- **Port Wine Tasting**: Cross to Vila Nova de Gaia for a guided tour and tasting at port wine cellars like Taylor's or Sandeman.

Day 3: Day Trip from Porto – Douro Valley

- **Douro Valley Tour**: Spend the day exploring Portugal's premier wine region. Book a guided tour or rent a car to visit picturesque vineyards, sample world-class wines, and take a scenic river cruise.
- **Lunch**: Enjoy a traditional Portuguese meal at a vineyard estate.
- **Evening Return**: Relax in Porto with a casual dinner at **Tapabento**, known for its creative tapas.

Day 4: Porto to Lisbon

Morning

- **Travel to Lisbon**: Take a scenic train ride (approximately 2.5-3 hours) or a short flight to Lisbon.
- **Check-In**: Choose accommodation in central neighborhoods like Baixa, Chiado, or Alfama.

Afternoon

- **Praça do Comércio**: Wander through Lisbon's grand riverside square, then explore nearby pedestrian streets.
- **Elevador de Santa Justa**: Ride this historic lift for sweeping views of Lisbon.

Evening

- **Fado Dinner**: Immerse yourself in Portuguese culture with a traditional Fado performance at a local restaurant, such as **Clube de Fado**.

Day 5: Exploring Lisbon

Morning

- **Belém District**: Visit the **Belém Tower** and the **Monastery of Jerónimos**, two UNESCO World Heritage Sites.
- **Pastéis de Belém**: Treat yourself to the world-famous custard tarts.

Afternoon

- **Alfama District**: Wander through the narrow streets, visit the **Lisbon Cathedral**, and stop at the **Miradouro da Senhora do Monte** for incredible city views.

Evening

- **Dinner**: Enjoy fine dining at **Cervejaria Ramiro**, known for its fresh seafood.

Day 6: Day Trip from Lisbon – Sintra and Cascais

- **Morning in Sintra**: Explore the fairytale-like **Pena Palace** and the mystical **Quinta da Regaleira**. Stroll through Sintra's charming town center.
- **Afternoon in Cascais**: Relax in this coastal town, visit the **Boca do Inferno** cliffs, or enjoy the sandy beaches.
- **Return to Lisbon**: Have a casual dinner at **Time Out Market** for diverse culinary options.

Day 7: Beaches and Farewell

Morning

- **Beach Time**: Visit **Costa da Caparica** or **Carcavelos Beach** for a relaxing morning by the sea.

Afternoon

- **Shopping and Souvenirs**: Head to Lisbon's **LX Factory** or **Chiado** district to pick up unique Portuguese handicrafts, tiles, or wine to take home.

Evening

- **Farewell Dinner**: End your trip at **Bairro do Avillez**, a restaurant by renowned chef José Avillez, for an unforgettable gastronomic experience.

Additional Tips

1. **Transportation**: Both cities are walkable, but public transportation (metros, trams, and buses) makes it easy to get around. Consider a travel card for savings.
2. **Packing**: Bring comfortable shoes for walking on cobblestone streets.
3. **Timing**: Adjust the pace to suit your preferences. This itinerary offers flexibility for longer stays at attractions or leisurely meals.

This week-long itinerary captures the heart of Portugal, offering a mix of history, culture, food, and relaxation. Enjoy your journey!

Family-Friendly Itineraries for Porto and Lisbon

Planning a family trip to Portugal? Porto and Lisbon are excellent destinations with plenty of attractions and activities to keep kids and adults entertained. Here's a family-friendly itinerary with a mix of cultural exploration, outdoor activities, and downtime to ensure everyone has a memorable experience.

4-Day Family Itinerary

Day 1: Arrival in Porto

- **Morning:** Arrive and check into a family-friendly hotel like HF Ipanema Park or Mercure Porto Centro Aliados.
- **Afternoon:** Stroll along the Ribeira District, explore the Douro Riverfront, and enjoy a family meal at a riverside café.
- **Evening:** Take a short Douro River Cruise for spectacular views. Many tours are kid-friendly, with comfortable seating and snacks.

Day 2: Exploring Porto

- **Morning:** Visit the World of Discoveries Museum, an interactive space where kids can learn about Portugal's Age of Exploration.
- **Afternoon:** Take the family to Jardins do Palácio de Cristal (Crystal Palace Gardens) for a picnic and to let the kids play in the open spaces.
- **Evening:** Enjoy dinner at Casa Virtude, which offers a warm, family-friendly atmosphere.

Day 3: Train to Lisbon and Belém District

- **Morning:** Take an early train to Lisbon (about 3 hours) and check into a family-friendly hotel like Novotel Lisboa or Martinhal Lisbon Chiado Family Suites.
- **Afternoon:** Head to the Belém District to visit the Belém Tower and Pastéis de Belém for some kid-approved treats.
- **Evening:** Relax with dinner at Time Out Market, which has a variety of food stalls to suit all tastes.

Day 4: Alfama and Kid-Friendly Fun

- **Morning:** Explore the Lisbon Oceanarium, one of Europe's largest aquariums, perfect for kids of all ages.
- **Afternoon:** Take a tram ride through the Alfama District and stop at family-friendly viewpoints like Miradouro da Senhora do Monte.
- **Evening:** Wrap up your trip with a fun meal at Hard Rock Cafe Lisbon, which caters to families with a casual vibe.

7-Day Family Itinerary

Day 1: Arrival in Porto

- Relax and settle into your accommodation. Spend time exploring the Ribeira District and enjoy dinner overlooking the Douro River.

Day 2: Porto Exploration

- Morning: Visit the SEA LIFE Porto Aquarium, an engaging spot for young kids.
- Afternoon: Head to Livraria Lello, and while parents enjoy the architecture, there's a children's section for young readers.
- Evening: Dinner at a casual, family-friendly restaurant like Tapabento.

Day 3: Douro Valley Day Trip

- Join a family-friendly Douro Valley tour. Some providers offer itineraries suitable for kids, with shorter boat rides and stops at scenic viewpoints.

Day 4: Travel to Lisbon

- Take a morning train to Lisbon. After settling in, spend the afternoon at Gulbenkian Garden, where kids can enjoy nature trails and ducks in the pond.

Day 5: Belém and Maritime Adventures

- Visit the Padrão dos Descobrimentos (Monument to the Discoveries) and the Belém Tower.
- Stop by the Maritime Museum, where interactive exhibits will keep the kids entertained.

Day 6: Alfama and Fun Activities

- Spend the morning at Lisbon Zoo, where kids can take a cable car ride over the animal enclosures.
- Afternoon: Ride the famous Tram 28 and explore Lisbon's historic streets.

Day 7: Beach Day

- Take a day trip to Costa da Caparica or Carcavelos Beach, where kids can play in the sand, and parents can relax. Return to Lisbon in the evening for a farewell family dinner.

Additional Family Tips

1. **Transportation:** Both cities have easy-to-use public transportation, and many trams and trains are stroller-friendly.
2. **Dining:** Restaurants are generally family-friendly, and high chairs are widely available. Many places offer kid-sized portions.
3. **Accommodations:** Look for hotels with family suites or rental apartments with kitchen facilities for added convenience.
4. **Pace:** Leave plenty of room for downtime, especially for younger children. Parks and open spaces are excellent for breaks.

With this family-friendly itinerary, you can ensure a balance of fun, relaxation, and discovery for every member of your group!

Useful Websites and Apps For Traveling to Portugal

Portugal has an abundance of digital resources to make your trip easier and more enjoyable. From booking accommodations to navigating cities, these websites and apps are indispensable for first-time and seasoned travelers. Here's a list of essential tools and a guide on how to use them effectively.

Transportation Apps

1. **Google Maps**

   - **What It Does**: Offers real-time navigation, public transportation schedules, and walking routes.
   - **How to Use**: Enter your destination, select your preferred mode of transportation (walking, public transit, or driving), and follow turn-by-turn directions. Download offline maps for Lisbon and Porto in advance.

2. **Moovit**

   - **What It Does**: Specializes in public transportation, offering detailed schedules, route planning, and service updates.
   - **How to Use**: Input your destination, and Moovit will suggest the best transit options, including bus, metro, and tram routes.

3. **CP - Comboios de Portugal**

- What It Does: Allows you to check schedules and book tickets for trains across Portugal.
- How to Use: Download the app or visit the website. Choose your departure and arrival cities, select travel times, and purchase tickets directly through the app.

4. **Bolt**

    - What It Does: A ride-hailing service similar to Uber, often cheaper and widely used in Portugal.
    - How to Use: Open the app, enter your destination, and request a ride. You can pay via the app using a credit card or opt for cash in some locations.

Accommodation Websites and Apps

1. **Booking.com**

    - What It Does: Offers a wide selection of accommodations, from budget hostels to luxury hotels.
    - How to Use: Search for stays in Porto or Lisbon by entering your travel dates. Use filters like "family-friendly" or "free cancellation" to narrow your options.

2. **Airbnb**

    - What It Does: Provides vacation rentals, including apartments and unique stays like farmhouses or villas.
    - How to Use: Search for properties by location, check reviews, and communicate directly with hosts for any specific requirements.

3. **Hostelworld**

    - What It Does: Specializes in affordable hostels and dormitory stays.
    - How to Use: Search for hostels in your destination, read reviews, and book dormitory or private rooms.

Local Information and Activities

1. **Visit Portugal**

   - **What It Does**: The official tourism website of Portugal, offering detailed guides, events, and insider tips.
   - **How to Use**: Browse by city or type of activity (e.g., culture, gastronomy). Download guides or maps for free.

2. **GetYourGuide**

   - **What It Does**: Helps you book guided tours, activities, and tickets for attractions.
   - **How to Use**: Enter your destination and travel dates, browse available experiences, and book tickets directly.

3. **Tiqets**

   - **What It Does**: Allows you to purchase tickets for museums, landmarks, and events, often with skip-the-line options.
   - **How to Use**: Search for specific attractions like the Belém Tower or Livraria Lello, and complete the purchase. Show the digital ticket at the entrance.

Dining and Food

1. **TheFork (formerly Zomato)**

   - **What It Does**: A restaurant discovery and reservation app, offering reviews, menus, and deals.
   - **How to Use**: Search for restaurants near your location, check reviews, and reserve a table directly through the app.

2. **Uber Eats**

   - **What It Does**: Food delivery from a wide variety of local restaurants.
   - **How to Use**: Enter your delivery address, browse restaurants, place your order, and track it in real-time.

Language and Communication

1. **Google Translate**

    - **What It Does**: Translates text, speech, and even images in real-time.
    - **How to Use**: Type or speak a phrase, or use your camera to translate text on signs or menus. Download the Portuguese language pack for offline use.

2. **Duolingo**

    - **What It Does**: A language-learning app perfect for picking up basic Portuguese phrases.
    - **How to Use**: Practice daily lessons before your trip to learn essential vocabulary and phrases.

Money and Budgeting

1. **XE Currency**

    - **What It Does**: Provides live currency exchange rates and allows for offline conversion.
    - **How to Use**: Input the amount in your currency, and it will show the equivalent in euros (EUR). Save the exchange rate for offline use when traveling.

2. **Revolut**

    - **What It Does**: A digital banking app offering multi-currency accounts, real-time currency exchange, and easy money management.
    - **How to Use**: Set up an account, add money, and use the app for secure payments in euros.

Emergency Services and Health

1. **112 Portugal**

    - **What It Does**: The official emergency app providing quick access to emergency numbers and services in Portugal.
    - **How to Use**: Open the app in case of an emergency to call the appropriate service (police, ambulance, fire department).

2. **Glovo**

    - **What It Does**: A delivery app that can bring essentials like groceries, medications, or even forgotten items to your location.
    - **How to Use**: Select your location, choose the type of delivery, and pay through the app.

Wi-Fi and Connectivity

1. **WiFi Map**

    - **What It Does**: A crowdsourced app that provides locations of free and password-protected Wi-Fi hotspots.
    - **How to Use**: Open the app, search for nearby hotspots, and follow the instructions to connect.

2. **Vodafone Portugal**

    - **What It Does**: Offers prepaid SIM cards and eSIM options for tourists.
    - **How to Use**: Visit a Vodafone store or kiosk at the airport, purchase a tourist plan, and activate it on your device.

Tlips for Using These Apps

- **Download Beforehand**: Ensure you have these apps downloaded and set up before you arrive in Portugal.
- **Offline Mode**: Use apps that offer offline functionality, like Google Maps, Google Translate, and XE Currency.
- **Language Settings**: Most apps are available in English, but familiarize yourself with key Portuguese terms just in case.

These apps and websites are indispensable tools to make your trip smooth and enjoyable, whether you're navigating the cities, finding places to eat, or booking experiences!

Printed in Great Britain
by Amazon